A Philosophy for Adult Education

A PHILOSOPHY

for

Adult Education

PAUL BERGEVIN

Emile

THE SEABURY PRESS · NEW YORK

PREFACE

This book has been written in order to articulate some ideas that constitute a supporting structure for a program of adult education in a free society.

Adult education is not a fad or a pastime of an affluent society. It is an ingredient so important to a social order struggling to be free that the success of the order is related directly to what the adult knows and how he practices what he knows.

In every society and in every institution making up that society the adult makes the decisions. While the education of every member of any social order is important, the quality of the society will not usually exceed the educational level of the adults who run it. Children's education is important, but the strong emphasis on it over the years has made many adults believe that the education they got as children and youths, plus a little experience along the way, is enough to carry them through the vicissitudes of adult life. The one big, or maybe not so big, educational meal taken as children can hardly be expected to sustain us through a lifetime full of challenge and change and adjustment.

The privileges and rights of a free people are dearly earned and are fragile. Opportunities for growth and development of the human mind and body and spirit are not available in a social order whose members are suppressed by political or religious bigots. An intelligent citizen actively participating in his society can effectively maintain and further a kind of social order that helps citizens mature and contribute to the civilizing process. Such intelligent action depends upon knowledge.

Because adult education can help us become knowledgeable, it must be made available to everyone, in a variety of ways, at different times and places. No one right solution for all our problems can be reached by any particular kind of adult education. A great variety of adult learning opportunities must be provided through all kinds of institutions: factories, libraries, schools, churches, clubs. Resources for learning, such as books, newspapers, radio and television, must be widely disseminated. Every adult must be continually exposed to the issues of the day and to ways of helping to solve them through active participation in some areas of his society. There are many ways to do the job. Adults do not all have to go to school every night, but we do need some elevating relationship with people and ideas so we can realize at least a part of our great potential and move toward personal and social fulfillment.

Adult education should be everyone's concern. It is important that a philosophy for the education of adults be considered by all thoughtful persons who wish to assume their share of responsibility for the kind of social order they live in. While the professional adult educator should play an important role in this field of activity, it is not an enterprise limited to his talents alone. Actually, most of the work in adult education is carried on by persons who have had little or no professional training in the problems of the education of the adult.

The volunteer worker in adult education is indispensable. Many persons are being paid to assume the responsibilities of conducting programs of adult education who have had little training in the discipline and have had to learn as they carried on. Yet these people have made substantial contributions to the field of adult education.

If adult education is everyone's concern, then we should

all be interested in doing something about it, and we should know why we are doing it. Further, we should care about ideas that will help us discover and utilize productively the great reservoir of human talent extant. It is hoped that this book may reveal such ideas and be helpful to persons who are willing to dedicate a part of their talent and time to the ever-present struggle to liberate the human mind from the fears and hates and suspicions that keep us from becoming whole, mature human beings.

The author is well aware that this work would not have been possible without the help of many of his students and associates in the teaching profession. To these persons he is grateful, as well as to the many people with whom he has worked in mental and general hospitals, prisons, churches, industry, and agriculture.

P. B.

CONTENTS

A Philosophy for Adult Education

INTRODUCTION

While there are clearly many areas of sameness among adults everywhere, there are also areas of difference such as the unique human characteristics that provide interest and zest in our association with one another. These human differences vary. Some make living an experience of never-ending interest and wonder; others tend to negate our struggle to achieve a richer civilization.

It should not be surprising, then, that philosophies of adult education can and do vary because of the people involved, the place, and the time. This does not mean that these philosophies have nothing in common, for they all concern the central area of relationship from which human development radiates; on the other hand, it does not mean that any one philosophy is necessarily as good as another. It would, however, be pretentious to think of one philosophical base of adult education as so universal in character as to be called *the* philosophy of adult education.

Assuming that one purpose of any philosophy is to establish a common point of reference, an integrated viewpoint, toward certain beliefs, ideas, attitudes, and practices, then what follows here can properly be called *a* philosophy of adult education.

The general concepts and underlying principles used here were first theoretically projected and then had their applicability tested. They have been derived, over a period of twenty years, partly from theory and partly from practice. They are now set forth because they can be translated into useful operational techniques. Experience has shown that they can be adapted to particular programs of adult learning. We have also tried to provide the creative educator with an integrated viewpoint that will assist him in interpreting general ideas and experiences for his particular situation.

The philosophy advanced here recognizes the value of preserving the uniqueness of individuals and groups within a reasonably disciplined social context. It allows for and promotes ways of preserving the differences we need in order to live and grow. When properly channeled, different opinions, beliefs, customs, and habits are as vital to human psychological and social growth as variety in diet is to physiological health.

To make true use of our particular talents we who are learners must be intimately involved, to different degrees and in different ways, in the entire learning process. We must learn how to participate effectively and must do so. We must learn that how we are taught is as important as what we are taught. We must learn to feel responsible for the success of the learning adventure by becoming involved in the dynamics of the adult learning process.

Adult education also has an important general purpose: to discover and present to the adult the opportunity to advance as a maturing individual, and to help him learn how to contribute his share to the civilizing process. This purpose would seem to offer an opportunity to the learner and the teacher to think of the adult as a unique human being with possibilities and limitations, constructive and destructive tendencies, capable of socially acceptable and antisocial acts, and able, to a degree, to become the good and virtuous person Aristotle describes in his *Politics*.

This philosophy of adult education basically points toward

4

the use of adult education for the development of free, creative, and responsible persons in order to advance the human maturation process. Adult learning programs carefully prepared to meet real human needs may play an important role in successfully exploiting our learning potential so that we become the mature persons it is possible for us to become.

If we are to realize our potential, the adult learning process must become a creating, releasing experience rather than a dulling series of passively attended indoctrination exercises.

In summary, the philosophy of adult education in this book is based upon the belief that:

1. Adult behavior can be changed to some extent;
2. Adult education should be designed to help people to grow up, mature;
3. Adults must be offered and helped to use the opportunity to act responsibly in the several facets of their adult lives: political, vocational, cultural, spiritual, and physical;
4. Adults should assume the obligation to learn to become more productive citizens;
5. Adults have untapped resources of creative potential that should be utilized;
6. Every conscious adult can learn;
7. Every adult can be helped to make better use of his intellectual capacity;
8. Adults need to live together in community in order to grow and mature, and they need to learn how to do this;
9. Every adult should find some way to express himself constructively and creatively;
10. Traditional teaching procedures and learning facilities are often inadequate;
11. An understanding of freedom, discipline, and responsibility promotes the discovery and productive use of our talents;

12. Such vital concepts as freedom, discipline, and responsibility can be comprehended by experiencing them through a variety of inspired learning experiences in a host of subjects;

13. What is called a free or democratic society must strongly emphasize lifelong learning for all its citizens, if they propose to remain free and to use their freedoms effectively;

14. Each adult participating in a learning experience should have the opportunity to help diagnose, plan, conduct and evaluate that experience along with his fellow learners and administrators;

15. The civilizing process is evolutionary and will advance in proportion to the number and intellectual quality of the adults who play an active role in that process;

16. Many adults associate education only with school. Adult learning that can cause behavioral change can take place at home, in church, in a factory, on a farm, in any place;

17. The means are as important as the ends;

18. The nature of man is neither "good" nor "bad," but he is essentially an adaptable, educable person in a state of becoming as well as being and capable of a degree of excellence he rarely attains. There is room for individual action and will in his struggle for achievement;

19. Behavior is conditioned by feelings and emotions as well as by reason and rational judgment;

20. Human beings seek fulfillment or happiness;

21. Adult education can help condition persons to live in a society and at the same time sensitize them to ways in which that society can be improved;

22. Up to the present the democratic idea has seemed to fit the nature of man and also of adult education as described in this book.

CHAPTER I

The Adult, His Society, and
Adult Education: An Overview

Our environment and the way we relate to it have much to do with making us the kind of persons we are. Talking with others, listening to the radio, watching television, reading, attending formal classes and lectures, traveling, even getting bawled out by the boss—all these experiences leave their marks on us and change us in one way or another. It is difficult to think of anything we do that does not either encourage our development toward maturity or thwart it.

The term "maturity" is used here to mean the growth and development of the individual toward wholeness in order to achieve constructive spiritual, vocational, physical, political, and cultural goals. A maturing person is continually advancing toward understanding and constructive action in the movement from mere survival (the state of lower animals) to the discovery of himself both as a person and as a responsible member of the social order.

1. THE CIVILIZING PROCESS

This action of the environment through society on the individual becomes, when positive, what we call the civilizing process. This developmental and evolutionary activity of society continually exposes us to the best of traditional and contemporary social experiences and teaches us how to relate to one another with understanding, dignity, and love. It should promote mature rationality in the lives of each of us and in our institutions.

The civilizing process is a corporate, social movement involving the whole of society, as it moves from barbarism toward refinement in behavior, tastes, and thought. It is also an evolutionary movement, one aimed toward further discovery and implementation of the human capabilities that will help us realize the kind of happiness achieved through "the pursuit of excellence," which Aristotle prescribes for "the good life."

An individual cannot really become a person outside the social order. The civilizing process contributes to the maturing individual and he, in turn, shares with others in making the civilizing process possible. This personal development contributes to the forward thrust of the civilizing process, making it a truly social movement. It also helps realize the corporate, social potential of the maturation process.

If an adult is to contribute to the civilizing process, he must know the direction in which society is moving in specific as well as in broad terms. As far as he is able, he must know what society is, what its general objectives are, and what he can do—culturally, vocationally, physically, politically, or spiritually—to assist in maintaining and furthering social objectives. He must also be aware of the responsibility society has for the individual, and the individual for society. This view is based on the assumption, supported in this book, that the individual is a member of a society that struggles to release him from his external as well as his self-imposed limitations and restrictions. Sometimes individuals do not wait for society to release them from these limitations, but they try to release themselves and others by assuming responsibility for disciplined and intelligent social action. On the other hand, there are always influences that retard the growth and progress of individuals and society. Again, some of these influences may be self-imposed, others may be social. Sometimes it is hard to distinguish one type from another.

Such things as value systems, the corporate nature of society, personal responsibility and privilege, and the nature of the individual and the group must be understood and dealt with by each of us according to his ability. No person can feel free from the responsibility of trying to extract some meaning from these terms. Those who are "educated" or in positions of educational, political, ecclesiastical, or economic authority are not solely responsible for carrying the full load. It would be undesirable if they did. History has many illustrations of people failing to assume responsibility in their role as thoughtful citizens. Such failures usually result in calls for quick action, and the ever-ready demagogue pops up to speed the process of political and social change.

Therefore, we as adults need to know. We need to act intelligently on what we know. We need to learn to discipline ourselves, to accept responsibility for, and to have something to say about some of the forces that shape us.

At the beginning of this chapter, we observed that it is difficult to think of any experience that does not influence our development in some way. Adult education in its broad sense can be said to include all those experiences, and they can be called "educational" because they modify, change, or reinforce our behavior in some way. In this very broad sense adult education can have negative as well as positive influences on us.

In its specific sense, however, adult education is a consciously elaborated program aiding and reinforcing the civilizing process. The over-all aim of the professional or lay adult educator, then, will be to bring each of us into some kind of constructive relationship with the civilizing process, always remembering that this process should represent those positive elements in environment and society that help us develop mature rationality in our lives and institutions.

We can be taught to hate other people and develop a quantitative value system, or we can be taught to love and to contribute to a value system that places quality in a sensible perspective with quantity. The quantitative idea tends to promote a society based on materialism and on a mechanization of thought and action in which the person becomes subordinated to the group and to the mechanical things he possesses and produces. The other idea seeks out and promotes human welfare through continually incorporating "the nature of things" into the civilizing process. Either idea can be promoted through the education of adults. It would be short-sighted, then, to consider adult education good or bad, *per se*.

We are all baffled by the complexities of our nature as well as by the seemingly endless complications of other natural phenomena. A favorite way of trying to escape the reality of complication is to develop some single purpose that can fit our finite concepts. Scarcely any area of study or investigation has escaped this snare. Actually, it's easier if grandpa, or the clergy, or our teachers classify and simplify for us; then all we have to do is remember the information and pass it on to others at appropriate times.

Related to the single-purpose idea is our penchant for placing everything in a good or bad category. Education is good. People ought to get a lot of it—when they are young. After you've been to school, you don't need anymore. Education is like the residual insect sprays, only the effect supposedly lasts longer.

Adult education can be truly "good" in that it can help

us to see ourselves, to develop, to relate our particular talents and abilities to the job of living, and to take our rightful places as maturing citizens in the civilizing process. Adult education can be "bad." It can teach us to love ourselves more than we love others; it can teach us to follow the demagogue without question; it can help us develop ideas and learn skills necessary to produce products or situations that can enslave or destroy us.

Adult education must, then, have a purpose greater than that of learning the skills of the craftsman and the physician and the entrepreneur, important as those are. If we are truly engaged in the maturity process, we do not live to work and make money, or have a physician keep us alive merely to be alive. We learn what to do with our lives, how to use our money and our good health to enrich our lives. We use these resources, money and education and health, to help us live. A significant task of adult education is to teach us how to live a full, productive life in which the ability to make a living and stay well is important, but equally important is the knowledge of what to do culturally and spiritually with our lives and talents.

Some of us believe that if everyone were exposed to the "truths" revealed in the view of education or religion or politics we hold, the problems of society would be solved. We often try to press upon others the ideas we know most about, or are able to understand, or believe we understand. But if we were to broaden our knowledge, we might give some credence to the views and customs of other persons.

Vocational educators and those concerned with liberal arts are both disturbed about what each considers the short-sighted views of the other. History is filled with examples of persons in power who display a singleminded devotion to some cult, and who are restless until they convert or "liberate" those who do not understand them or disagree with them. We need to understand the views of others and might possibly use some of this new-found knowledge to enrich our own. Systems developed by human beings inevitably contain some of the deficiencies of their developers.

The vigorous presentation of different ideas gives a vitality to society which is essential to its survival and its advancement as a maturing organism. When we are forced, either subtly or overtly, to follow certain ideas blindly, we lose those helpful values that might exist within the ideas themselves; for we have not been given the freedom we need to come into an understanding relationship with the ideas according to our own abilities.

The subject areas of economics, philosophy, history, psychology, literature, languages, and the sciences are of prime importance in some phases of adult education. It would be of great value if all adults could be offered and would accept the opportunity to participate in well-operated programs involving the best of the past and the present represented in those fields.

Some programs of adult education presently include these vital, broad areas of learning on a basis appropriate to the development of the adult as a maturing, participating member of an evolving society rather than as a part of a separatist movement emphasizing snob-appeal.

Much work must be done in the field of adult education to bring the great stores of information contained in the arts and sciences into intimate relationship with the adult learner. Special programs must be developed to expose adults to other cultures through languages, philosophy, history, geography, ecology, sociology, and so on. These areas must be developed to show a relationship to the adult's own needs and to show what is meant by such ideas as responsibility for one another, freedom, discipline, and a free society.

These subjects certainly encompass funds of knowledge that can be focused on adult living. But they are too often taught to adults as subjects, "just as we do in college. If you want it, here it is. If you can't get it, that's too bad." *Most adults are not scholars and they aren't interested in becoming scholars.* Adult learning programs must take this fact into consideration.

Children have to attend school; adults don't, usually, and most of them won't unless they can see some advantage in it. Our adult educational ideas must be adapted to these facts. Whether we like it or not, everybody needs to be exposed to learning, not for learning's sake but for humanity's sake. The content of the learning must be broad and appropriate to the variety of objectives pursued. Sometimes what we think of as subjects—history, mathematics, art, etc.— are useful. Many times programs of learning should be developed around the particular problems and needs of the participants.

Freedom is necessary to give each of us a chance to find himself, a chance to live a life in keeping with his unique personality. Encumbrances often make it difficult, if not impossible, for us to discover our potential and the degree of happiness that could come from the effective exploitation of it. Many persons believe that freedom is in the nature of things, a human need that must be understood and utilized if we are to mature, to develop, to grow.

It is also in the nature of things for us to be grasping and ego-centered. Our nature makes us compassionate and sociocentered when directed along those lines or revengeful and capable of destruction when trained in that direction. Since reason is a device often used to justify our views and behavior, it is at the mercy of the reasoner. We have the faculty of making almost anything sound right.

Our many-sided nature gives rise to many capabilities and resulting behaviors. We have what we choose to call our better nature. It conforms to a degree and directs its energy to the established social views and patterns; and we

13

have our darker side, which is the antithesis of this view. When we speak of the nature of things, we think of conditions as they actually are—good, bad, and indifferent. Our nature is composed of these qualities. Nature is nature and, of itself, defies categorization into good and bad. It is up to us to select, to discover our potential, and to utilize it within the limits of our particular natures and of the environment in which we find ourselves. We have discovered many interesting and valuable facts about ourselves. We know that we can love and we can hate, that we need freedom and discipline, that we are ambitious and lazy, that we are ego-centered and socio-centered, and that we have many other characteristics that contribute to our ambivalent feelings.

Perhaps the most important thing we have ever discovered in our nature is that we can learn. We can learn to cope with some of the conflicts and ambivalences that seem to be a part of the natural order. We can learn both to care for ourselves and to see to it that those less fortunate are helped to learn to lead a useful life, or made more comfortable if they are unable to be productive. We have learned that we must do something, that our energy and talent must be expended in one direction or another. It is just as natural for this talent and energy to be expended in anti-social acts as it is in deeds that will further desirable patterns of personal and social behavior.

In truth, the continuing education of adults is not a leisure-time activity, nice if one has the time for it. It is the determining factor in the race between building and destroying, between the civilizing process and barbarism. We adults are capable of either and both.

We claim to prefer the civilizing process. While we have many differing views on how this is to be accomplished, most of these views have similar ends: to discover and satisfy human needs, to liberate human kind, to give us an opportunity to become the kind of creatures we ought to become.

14

When there is a race, there is a winner and a loser. While the race is still going on, the opportunity to make one's support felt on either side still exists. The support the civilizing effort needs can be supplied by tens of millions of adults who are willing to try to learn to carry their share of the social load and to identify and develop the part of their nature that leads toward maturing citizenship.

These goals require continuous effort. The adult who believes that having been to school when he was younger will suffice so far as learning is concerned is a social liability. Of course, schools aren't the only places people can learn. Actually, the schools should teach people how to learn, using subjects as examples and vehicles of learning. Learning can take place anywhere, and one kind or another does. But the kind of learning that helps us become increasingly mature, that helps us identify our personal and corporate problems and handle them intelligently—this is the kind of learning that can improve the chances of the civilizing process being the winner.

To hope that we can get along with what we have learned in school, regardless of how far we went, is about as futile as if we were to place a small sum of money in a bank and expect it to last the rest of our lives. In the case of the money and the bank, it is clear that we would soon be broke and then, if we failed to go to work, would become public charges.

Many of us are, indeed, social public charges, even though we are making our way financially. We are making injudicious decisions, misleading people, and making choices based on prejudices, misinformation, and half-assimilated facts. We can never have all the information we need; we can not always be right; but we can learn to do a better job than we now do. Only when we begin to show as much enthusiasm for the continuing education of every adult citizen as we do for our children's education can we expect realistic results.

15

To participate effectively in a free society an adult must learn to do a good job vocationally; he must have some kind of spiritual support; he must know something of the world of which he is a part and his culture; he must know something of himself and his fellow man. All this requires learning, and the learning acquired in school is not sufficient to hold a person for life. Such social concepts as freedom and political equality can become nothing more than platitudes, unless a large portion of the populace in what is called a democracy has the understanding and integrity to interpret these principles intelligently and relate them to responsible citizenship. The nature of a society and its success as a liberating force depend on the ability of its citizens to understand and support social concepts like freedom and equality.

2. Choosing a Direction for Adult Education

If we are seriously concerned with developing and maintaining an effective adult education program that will help us relate better to ourselves and to the world about us, we will have to direct it toward a purpose and design the program to suit the purpose. Generally we like to do what has been done rather than change, but in some human endeavors we cause change to take place faster than we can learn to adjust to it. Particularly in the sciences, changes are taking place at a phenomenal rate, not in the way the subjects are taught but in the content itself. In the complex areas of learning how to live and make proper use of our talents, the changes are not so rapid. In many instances, the methods being used to "enlighten" mankind are the same ones used several hundred years ago when most of us were peasants. A major difference is that in the past only a few had books and time; now both educational materials and leisure time are available to large numbers of people. Most persons who wish to do independent study can make productive use of their leisure time and take advantage of the materials available from many sources: public libraries, newsstands, book-stores, universities and colleges, private libraries (unions, churches, clubs, etc.).

The change in how adults are taught has been negligible. But the social change has been tremendous. One obvious example of social change is in the political order. A few centuries ago a handful of people ran everything; today increasing numbers of people are involved in most decisions made. And the fact that more of us are not involved in decision-making today is, to a large extent, the result of our indifference or unwillingness to assume responsibility rather than of the political system under which we live. The political machinery is available, but we either do not wish to make full use of our opportunities to participate or we do not know how to do so.

Clear-cut changes are necessary to live in today's world. Indeed, this has been the case in an evolving world since time began. More and more of us must be encouraged to share responsibility for the work we do, the church we worship in, and the state we belong to. Since more of us must be involved and many of us are lethargic, we must come to grips with a kind of learning that will accomplish the desired results. It is not just a matter of selling adults the idea that they need more learning and should take a lot of "courses" as they did in school so that by some mysterious process they will learn what they and society need to know. Some adults are involved in adult education and feel they are "learning something." They should continue. Millions are not involved in any kind of regular, organized learning program. If the present social experiment is to survive and improve, this situation will need to be corrected, since democracy depends on an educated citizenry.

We have a choice between two alternatives as a base upon which this vast and needed program of adult education—cultural, physical, political, vocational, and spiritual—should operate:

1. We can indicate that we have an unalterable "truth," use educational processes to propagate this "truth," and by one means or another bring the learner to a prearranged conclusion.

2. We can indicate that truth is complex, evolving, and difficult to come by; that facts are learned differently by different people because people are different; that sometimes the learner may have to learn to be as comfortable as he can in what might be called a state of suspension, because he cannot wholly accept or completely understand what is to be learned.

What are the results to the learner of each of these bases for a program of education of adults?

In the first instance, the propagation of facts or truths chosen by administrators or leaders is an instrument used extensively in many social institutions. Some of our most powerful opinion-forming agencies proclaim they have a truth and indicate that the learner need only understand it, believe it, and become a follower. The real thinking has been done for him. It remains for him to memorize and accept the "facts" so he can become a respected and tractable member of his political party, union, class in school, church, vocation, lodge, or whatever.

There may well be actual facts and truths in the organization that would clearly help the learner reconcile himself to realities, become a more efficient and skillful worker, or assume more responsibility for the conduct of the human community. But, if the learner is to be helped to grow, to mature, to develop into the kind of person he could become, he must exercise his own talents whether they are little or great. When we are asked to assume responsibility for a job, a family, or a position in our community, we cannot be expected to be very effective if we have had little or no chance to practice assuming responsibility. Yet often more

18

is expected of us than we are able or willing to give. When we've been taught most of our lives to listen and learn facts from those who know, we will naturally wait for someone who knows to tell us how to do everything. We will not try even feebly to learn to do something ourselves in our own unique way and try, at the same time, to fit that uniqueness into the need of the social group. We are products of how we have been taught to think, and most of us don't take the trouble to think too much, partly because everywhere we find persons who will do the thinking for us. In government those "in the know" have to get the people ready for war or for an attack on problems of disease or education. This means that persons skilled in the art of propaganda are usually the successful politicians. The people are too frequently persuaded to the politician's point of view rather than forming an enlightened populace represented by the politician.

There exists today no more poignant example of successfully ramming "facts" down people's throats on a massive scale than that accomplished by some professional advertisers. These persons have made a highly rewarding financial game out of contributing, in many cases, to a reversal of the human maturation process. Mass media, which can contribute to the civilizing process, are being used to neutralize independent thinking. Lack of responsibility for the public weal demonstrated by the modern television industry is a case in point. Such an opportunity for mass development of society as that given to television has rarely presented itself. More people can be reached more easily than had ever been thought possible. But for the most part, the opportunity of contributing to our maturity is being spent on drama (using the word in its loosest and broadest sense) and entertainment sandwiched between carefully developed and delivered instructions about soap, automobiles, hair grease, or tobacco—products the seller believes people should buy. Appeals by some corporations and their ad-

19

vertisers clearly select the weaknesses of human nature, those weaknesses that some organizations and groups are honestly trying to reduce.

Some years ago medicine shows traveled from one community to another telling people how to diagnose their ills and persuading them to buy their nostrums for sure cure. Today advertisers on television have refined some of the callous logic of the medicine show but retained the basic principle that the populace is naïve and, if psychologically prepared, will accept almost anything. Some devices capable of releasing humanity can also be employed to enslave it.

In the struggle to turn a fast buck some persons go beyond what even a rather benign public will accept, and society imposes controls on an ever-increasing scale. These people contribute to the destruction of a free society by being unable to understand or accept the degree of self-discipline concomitant with freedom.

Society could advance further than we can imagine if we could learn to use the facilities we have. As long as citizens are played for ignorant suckers and fast-buck materialism continues to be a large portion of our diet, just that long will we be engaged in a conflict to keep even, at most, in the struggle for human advancement.

We are victims of our own folly. We need each other's help to overcome our shortcomings, to lighten our way. It is true that we have done things we ought not to have done, and we are open to being misled. The cruel reality is that these shortcomings are used and preyed upon "legally."

These are real, vivid, and crucial reasons why adult education is neither good nor bad of itself. It depends on how it is used. Adults can be persuaded and taught to kill each other, to live beyond their means, to worry, to destroy themselves in many ways. Adults can also be educated to love each other, to help each other, to make sensible uses of the great resources nature bestows upon them, to make good use

20

of their time, talent and money, to enjoy a full and fruitful life through productive work, play, worship, and study.

Where adult education is turned to productive, fruitful uses, the adult learner must have a dynamic relationship with the process of learning. He must be a part of it and take part in it. He must participate. The alternative to this is the passive adult learner whose sole participation is being present and listening.

When a program of adult learning is based on the idea that "we have the truth and you'll be comfortable if you listen, learn, and do what those who know think should be done," the adult learner does not have a chance to exercise his judgment, he cannot practice discreet observations by questioning, he will not be able to participate in organized discussion because he doesn't know how. He can only ask questions of the authority to determine if he correctly understood him. He cannot grow and mature properly because he cannot give vent to that uniqueness within him through which he can learn in his own way.

This is a kind of adult teaching-learning based on the propagation of a captive idea or truth taught by repetition. The learner has little or nothing to say about what is happening to him. The disciplines of psychology, sociology, and education are sometimes used to develop and conduct programs of adult learning that neutralize or retard the adult maturation process. While modern advertising is a prime offender, it does not stand alone. Some of our most respected institutions also are guilty.

Learning is too often thought of as something that takes place in a classroom under the guidance of an instructor. Actually, most adult learning has nothing to do with a school or classroom. Learning that causes adults to change the ways they think or believe or behave takes place all the time, for good or for ill. Mass media, particularly television and radio, are constantly engaged in teaching us how to think about what they are selling; and fraternal organizations, churches, labor unions, etc., play their part in forming thought-patterns in the adult mind.

The television medicine man trying to make life more tolerable for hemorrhoid sufferers, the supervisor instructing the worker on the job, the dedicated churchman teaching the principles of religion—all these people are adult educators. Like scores of others in many other institutions, each of them is trying to change the way we think and behave and often succeeding. Although these institutions and organizations have various motives and various views of human kind to support their motives, they are all educating. They are doing something to the adult mind. Some of these educators promote maturity; some of them are irresponsible, well-meaning persons who merely promote, without giving much thought to what their ideas do for human advancement; others are concerned with their own ends, promoters who use people to accomplish those ends.

These adult educators are trying to advance some kind of truth. The learner need only come in contact with this truth by rote—learn it, believe it, don't question it, since this could undermine belief. While the honesty and dedication of some who use this way of propagating a truth are often sound, others use the same process to mislead and destroy. While serving different ends, both groups emphasize a degree of authority that often ignores the adult learner's need to inquire and question in order to grasp even sound and established truths.

The other base for a program of adult education, and the one supported in this book, considers truth complex and difficult to come by, sometimes evasive and relative. Truth is considered something sought for by everyone to some degree. In their own ways and according to their own abilities, all persons should have opportunities to seek knowledge and truth in their jobs, in the churches, and in their cultural and recreational activities. In a real, constructive

22

sense the job of the adult educator is to see that opportunities to study, discuss, and inquire are made available to the adult learner and to help the learner make use of those opportunities.

The statement that truth is hard to come by and is sometimes relative does not mean that there are no truths or that some things are not closer to truth than others. Further, this statement is not intended to convey the idea that all truth is relative or that a principle or point of view can be manipulated to justify any kind of idea or behavior. The truth of a thing does not depend on how a person looks at it. We must help each other see things as they are, rather than as we may think they are or ought to be.

We humans can reason ourselves into or out of anything. Benjamin Franklin aptly stated, "So convenient a thing it is to be a reasonable creature, since it enables one to find or make a reason for everything one has a mind to do."

Tradition plays a dynamic role in our behavior. Some traditions have helped us avoid certain error by making use of the wisdom and the mistakes of the past.

The literature of many centuries is filled with reports of social and psychological experiences of human kind which only a misanthrope would choose to ignore. Certain facts and truths produce certain results if society chooses to follow them. Other beliefs and ideas are in a suspended state and are being looked into by persons concerned with human behavior.

Full adult growth depends on how ideas are taught, on whether adults are encouraged to approach problems and truths as full partners in the learning process. Given this opportunity, they will attack the learning problem as full partners in the learning process, they will be truly contributing to the idea. They will learn the thrill of discovery and share the excitement that comes from free and disciplined creative inquiry.

Too often adult educators in schools, unions, churches,

agricultural groups and industries are concerned about getting the educational job done in a hurry. People have to learn certain facts about their job or their institution fast; speed is of the essence because there are so many people and so little time. Time is money, they say. Such slogans may produce more things, but this philosophy of speed does not necessarily produce quality human beings. It does often produce psychological and physiological problems which must be dealt with sooner or later. Speed, automation, the concentration of manufacturing industry, and the consequent urbanization of society are causing momentous social and psychological questions which we are either unaware of, unwilling to recognize, or unsure what to do about. Some of us think it almost unpatriotic either to admit or to try to solve some of the problems created by our struggle to surround ourselves with more things. Too often greed, ignorance, and passion direct us toward a symptomatic assault unworthy of our best efforts.

Many of the underlying problems causing strikes and other social conflicts are only partly related to the stated problems. We have to do something now and then besides our nightly sessions with beer and television and planning next year's vacation. We have to try to compensate for the boredom created by the industrialized social order. The more we become specialized, as lights flash and machines do our thinking and we become less needed, the more we try to find ways to establish ourselves in the new order. First we try socially acceptable ways; but, if society is not awakened to the seriousness behind these disturbances, then the struggle for survival of human dignity will take on more violent patterns.

It is highly unlikely that a people who have had a taste of freedom and who have been taught something about the value and dignity of the human being can be readily subjugated by either man or machine. But we can be subjugated in time. And the temptation to surrender can be increased by surrounding us with more money and things. If we can get our share of the booty, we tend to turn away from considering seriously the problems of the natural development and maturation of human kind.

Related to establishing a base and direction for the education of the adult is our general lack of concern for problems affecting our well-being. An example of this is the preservation of the natural resources that we need to survive: air and water, land and animal life. Nature's means of sustaining all life interests relatively few persons; and even fewer are actively trying to solve this problem.

Some of us are gaining financially by the kind of progress that covers our cities with smoke and noxious gases, that fills the atmosphere above us with shattering vibration and ear-splitting noise, that makes the water in our streams and rivers unfit for recreation or human consumption. Money is a drug for which no antidote has been found even in the present world of scientific achievement. Materialism can win and is presently making a good showing in the direction of victory.

Adult education has a job to do, a momentous task. It has more to do than teaching adults how to make more money. Leaders in adult education must examine long and carefully what society hopes to achieve.

Persons concerned with this important work must try above all else to use every legitimate facility that can help release the untapped potential in every human being. We must continually seek out and discover as much as we can about our nature and needs and how we fit into the nature of things. Programs of many descriptions must be developed to suit and advance the part of our nature that responds to the civilizing process. These programs must provide socially acceptable outlets as substitutes for some of our more barbaric inclinations and antisocial traits.

A great part of the problem of getting more adults involved in adult education programs suited to their needs comes from failure to understand certain ideas about the continuing education of adults. Many questions need to be understood and these understandings should be reflected in the learning programs carried on. Examples are: What is this program for? What are we trying to do? Who does it? When is it done? Why is it done? Where is it done? What results can be looked for? How long should it continue? How does it differ from the education of children?

Since social and individual development is characterized by change, the approach to problems of change in the education of the adult must be flexible. Adult education must be based on a philosophy of change, of movement. It must also take into account the nature of the adult as a learner, always learning something for his edification or his destruction. The adult can be stimulated to inquire, to try to discover, to be creative. If fear or shame are motivating factors, he can not engage productively in learning. He must be offered an opportunity to attack a problem in a way suited to his nature as a learner, at a level he can handle, in a manner (process) that helps him know more about working with others and himself as well as about a particular subject. Regardless of the subject—chemistry, history, better pasture grass, or religion today, every area of inquiry should include a valid and understood purpose for the study and a continuing opportunity to develop an understanding and working relationship with the learner and with his fellow learners.

When adult education existed mainly as random learning, when it was unnecessary for adults in general to know very much except how to follow orders, it was probably unnecessary to consider the problem of purpose in adult learning. Today we are in a different social environment from that of a hundred years ago, different in fact from any in recorded history. One of the great differences is political. For the first time on a large scale the average person has something to say about the social forces which make up his world. Influence of this kind is being felt in all major institutions. Irrespective of our feelings about it, the institutions where people worship and work and the institutions of government are aware that an increasing number of persons are demanding and getting more to say about the operation of those institutions. One known answer to the survival and vigorous extension of these institutions is the continuous education of the adults who take part in their operation.

Aristotle was not sure that large numbers of people would be willing to participate intelligently in democracy. He believed most of us would demand more and more, and politicians would rise to the occasion and compete with each other for the favor of the mob. He believed democracies promoted the idea that people should live as they liked and that most people preferred to live in a disorderly fashion.

A lot of things have happened since 350 B.C., but basically people have not changed very much. It may be well to heed the observations of Aristotle and avoid the pitfalls he points out if we wish to equip ourselves to assume the awful responsibilities presented to us as citizens of a democratic state.

When choosing between indoctrination or continually seeking truth, it seems reasonable to assume that the second choice will best fit the pursuit of a disciplined and reasonably free life. Truth is evolving and difficult to come by and we must be free enough to pursue it with a lively concern. It must not be handed to us from above as untouchable. Every one of us must be part of the teaching-learning process and learn, according to his ability, the meaning and proper use of discipline and participation in our continuous search to know.

CHAPTER II

Goals and Structure for Adult Education

A goal states the objectives to be attained, the ends to be reached, the results to be achieved. In order to establish educational goals we must ask such questions as: What do we expect to accomplish? When should this be done? Also, we must state our specific intentions. Goals vary in significance from such an all-encompassing goal as Aristotle's belief in the pursuit of excellence in order to achieve the good life to less weighty objectives, such as to learn to read Spanish within the next fourteen months. But in every situation where some accomplishment is to be realized, a goal has to be considered carefully and stated understandably.

Much adult learning takes place without any recognizable or stated goal. Such random learning apparently occurs as a result of the mass media a citizen is exposed to, the general conversations he engages in, and similar unplanned learning experiences. But adult learning programs, in which definite and concrete results are expected, may not achieve the expectations of the participants unless they recognize some clearly stated, educationally attainable goal. The importance of goals will be treated later. At this point it is sufficient to state that a learning group would scarcely know where they were in a learning program if they didn't know, at the outset, where they intended to go. This seemingly obvious situation would not bear stating were it not that a large percentage of organized adult learning programs have either poorly delineated or unstated goals.

Goals vary with different people, different situations, and different things to be done. In the education of adults toward a creative fulfillment of their lives in a free society, certain goals are designed to further the social views that exist in this social order. In other societies different goals are designed to accomplish different ends.

1. Some Major Goals of Adult Education

The major goals of adult education expressed here will assist an adult to develop into the kind of person it is possible for him to be—a free, creative, responsible, productive, and maturing citizen. These goals should help him grow and develop as a contributing member of a social order that will in turn present him with continuing opportunities to fulfill his particular purpose in life.

Each major goal that follows emphasizes a pertinent element in the education of adults. Such goals can help differentiate between indoctrination and free, creative, disciplined learning. These goals help develop human kind. They are part of a dynamic, changing order of things and, therefore, some of them might be changed or adjusted as we learn more about ourselves and our relationships with other persons.

These goals are listed below, not necessarily in their order of importance. Each of them is then briefly treated:

a. To help the learner achieve a degree of happiness and meaning in life;

b. To help the learner understand himself, his talents and limitations, and his relationships with other persons;

30

c. To help adults recognize and understand the need for life-long learning;

d. To provide conditions and opportunities to help the adult advance in the maturation process spiritually, culturally, physically, politically, and vocationally;

e. To provide, where needed, education for survival, in literacy, vocational skills, and health measures.

(a) *To help the learner achieve a degree of happiness and meaning in life.* Somehow or other we try to seek out and follow some way of life which seems to provide us a kind of contentment or security with which we can live. Since so much of what is sought depends on the individual seeker —his knowledge, his emotional make-up, his physical stamina, and his ability to use what he has, we can easily understand that people seek different things or expect the same things to satisfy them in different ways. But somehow or other everyone tries to find a degree of comfort or contentment sometimes called happiness.

Some of us try drugs that temporarily change our body chemistry and offer a feeling of well-being. Alcoholic beverages, narcotics, and tobacco are often used to help us live, tolerate life, or satisfy our natural need for a feeling of well-being. Such satisfaction is delusory. No drug can provide a short-cut; there is no easy way. Drugs may enslave, but they will not release.

Some religious persons point out that happiness can never be fully attained on earth, that our place is with God in eternity, and that we are discontented and restless until this ultimate goal is reached. However, a degree of happiness can be achieved in our present state by following a path which leads to the ultimate goal.

One way or another we are seeking happiness, but what one person can relate to and derive satisfaction from may be anathema to another. Part of this difference is due to the life-long training each seeker has received.

Over the years of human habitation of the earth, many things have been learned and passed on to succeeding generations. We have been taught not only how to survive, but also how to develop our better nature through the civilizing process. Helping ourselves by helping each other is an example of an idea which many persons feel is in the nature of the human being. Striving to carry out such ideas helps to fulfill our purpose in life, and therefore gives us a feeling of satisfaction, of happiness.

Some ideas that evoke happiness can be taught to adults —not in charm courses, but through regular educational programs carried on by institutions. Personal achievement brings us satisfaction; so does helping and knowing other people; learning more about the world around us and where we fit into the picture helps bring meaning and purpose and fulfillment into our lives. The resulting satisfaction can well be termed happiness. Our experiences must be related to these ideas. This can be done through practically every adult learning program if the leaders, educators, or administrators are perceptive enough to see the importance of these concepts and will take time to incorporate them in the programs.

Misunderstanding of the idea of excellence has resulted in many emotional problems, some slight and some very serious. Excellence is defined by our capabilities and abilities. The parent who insists that his child be a winner at any cost or that he follow a program unsuited to the child's talent or wishes, is setting up potential emotional problems with which the child may not be able to cope successfully in later years. Being as good as you can be and being the best are quite different goals.

The pursuit of excellence gives meaning to our lives through whatever helps us extend our horizons, better identify and solve problems, sharpen our concern for others, and enjoy the excitement of new discoveries in the realms of ideas and situations.

We are made to be active, inquiring beings and our lives will find meaning as we learn about our nature and play our roles in a social order that encourages activity and growth. This pursuit of excellence can be a means of achieving fulfillment and happiness.

(b) *To help the learner understand himself, his talents and limitations, and his relationships with other persons.* Modern as well as ancient sages speak of the need for self-understanding in terms familiar to everyone. "Know thyself" and "the first look should be within" are familiar phrases. In most cases admonitions like these become so commonplace that they make little or no lasting impression. Like much of the information we deal with in adult education, the idea is not new. One of our problems is to understand and put to constructive use what we already know.

Most of the process of understanding ourselves falls under the heading of random experiential learning. Trial and error of a very informal nature is one way we deal with this learning problem. In recent years some persons have submitted to psychoanalysis in an effort to learn more about themselves, who they are, and why they are what they are. This costly and time-consuming method of learning is not available to most persons. Good literature has many examples of behavioral patterns carefully observed and delineated. Such information can help us understand our nature and the nature of our fellow men.

Regardless of how we learn it, we must learn to know ourselves. Our success in dealing with ourselves and others is closely related to how we know ourselves and what we are able to do with what we know. Knowing what we can and cannot do will help us make the most of what we have and prevent a costly waste of energy expended in areas unsuited to our talents.

Some time ago a popular song boldly proclaimed, "Anything You Can Do, I Can Do Better." While things like this amuse many people, some of us really believe we can do anything if we try hard enough. Disappointment and frustration too often reward those who are so unrealistic. Self-confidence and self-esteem are important factors in emotional health and success. We achieve them to the degree that we comprehend and stay within our limitations and identify and use our talents.

Adult education should be directed toward helping the learner become whole, toward helping to piece together the fragmented parts of his life into that unique working unit, the individual. Each of us has an important part to play in the social drama, and we have to learn what that part is, as well as how to play it. We can't very well learn our part in isolation. It is learned in relationship with others.

The attempt to understand ourselves should help to reveal our virtues and vices, our good and bad points, and our talents and limitations. From here we can start. We are in a position to do something about changing after we have seen the situation but not before. We can accomplish some of this change ourselves, but we also have to depend on our fellow humans to help. If we are really to learn, we have to recognize what we need to know. First, we must know something of ourselves.

We needn't be shocked, disappointed, or particularly overjoyed about what we see as we learn more about ourselves. We need to understand our humanity, taking as objective a look as we can, and then to start on the perpetual job of improving.

(c) *To help adults recognize and understand the need for life-long learning.* Rousseau tells us that man is born free, yet he is everywhere in chains. It is a dramatic statement. Man is probably just born, and the chains that bind him are partly of his own making and partly made by the times in which he lives, the general circumstances surrounding him, and the society of which he is a part. But he is a part of that society; and, if he is afforded the opportunity to have something to say about the constitution of it, he has, indeed, an opportunity to deal with some of the forces that shape his destiny. In Rousseau's time the opportunities of free expression were limited, and he could point to the social systems as major factors in the enslavement of human kind. Today we can accuse the system, but generally our accusations exhibit little more than an effort to shift responsibility, to hide our failure to face the tasks that are ours in a society that is trying to give ordinary people like us a chance to show if we can stand up to the challenge of being citizens.

Aristotle did not believe that people would fare too well under democracy. He believed people are guided by their own interest and show little concern for the common cause. They are easily swayed by first one demagogue, then another, and they are guided more by what they can get than by principle and order.

Hobbes saw us in a perilous position due to our nature. He thought people sought power and would finally choose to submit to a power in order to protect themselves from themselves.

The establishment and maintenance of order has occupied the minds of responsible social observers over many centuries. Some have had serious doubts that the idea of democracy was suited to our nature. There can be little doubt that, if democracy is to survive, citizens must participate intelligently in the affairs of the various institutions that constitute democratic society. And intelligent participation is predicated on learning.

Continuous education of one sort or another is not a luxury but a necessity. Education is a built-in requirement of a society emerging from control by the few to control by the many. We have yet to awaken to the fact that going to school as youngsters is not enough. Our present view gives only a perfunctory nod to adult education and puts a disproportionate emphasis on the education of youth. While the need for education of the young is acute, so is the need for continuing education of older people. Persons cannot continue to feed on the rights of a free society without knowing how to identify and share the responsibilities entailed in maintaining and extending these rights. This takes a kind of learning. Only as we learn to make discreet choices and take our fair share of the social load can we and others enjoy the fruits of this endeavor.

Adult education has as a major objective the job of trying to convince people of the importance of learning in a free society. Too many of us are apathetic and unconcerned about the commonweal. "Let the other fellow take care of himself; that's what I have to do," is not the valid cry of a citizen of a democracy. The other fellow has to work, if he can; but he may need to be taught how to do a job, how to assume responsibility, and what is expected of him by society. This is one of the many tasks of adult education. A citizen must know and act intelligently on what he knows, or somebody will act for him. Nature abhors a vacuum; in social as in physical vacuums, something will try to fill the gap. Someone will always come to the fore to tell us what to do and how and when to do it, and to take from us the burden of thinking and responsibility, only to replace it with one of submission.

Continuous learning of many subjects and the application of what we know can help us learn to participate in society. Knowing more about history, art, music, gardening, and politics can improve our ability to see the relative importance of things and their true relationship.

Adult education must not only provide opportunities for the education of adults; it must also help all adults understand the continuing and urgent need for adult learning in a free society.

36

(d) *To provide conditions and opportunities to help the adult advance in the maturation process spiritually, culturally, physically, politically, and vocationally.* Since we are part of a dynamic, changing, evolutionary drama, something is always happening to us. We are either advancing—developing and growing by trying to discover and use our potential, or we are retrogressing—using less and less of our talents. We are never standing still. We either use the part of our nature that bids us mature and grow up, or we fall prey to the idea that anything is good enough, that our contribution won't count anyway.

Institutions conducting adult education programs must establish conditions and present opportunities to make the maturation process understandable and attractive. Adult education can not be said to have fulfilled its mission unless it deals with the whole person. Learning programs are frequently directed to some highly specialized area. Little effort is made to see the adult in his struggle to become whole. Each institution is concerned with its own idea; this too often creates adults who are not taught to think, to weigh, or to evaluate, but rather to repeat what someone has said. Little wonder, then, that it is difficult for most of us to see both sides of an issue. We've been trained to see one side, the "right" side, and this kind of training makes us seek and be satisfied with a quick, neat, yes-or-no answer. Many of the problems with which adults deal do not fit into tidy patterns. Situations are often complex and answers tentative, and we have to learn to live with provisional solutions.

One institution will emphasize the spiritual development of the adult, another the vocational, and so on. We rarely find one that will take time to integrate its particular area of concern with the whole or with any other areas. The maturation process is thereby hindered. While it would be unrealistic to expect all areas in the make-up of a person to develop at the same rate and time, some movement or change in each area can give the learner a better understanding of the importance of relationships in the solution of problems.

Whoever conducts adult education programs should make sure each learner gets a chance to understand that our job is to progress from immaturity to maturity and that this process involves several related facets of an individual's life. Each of these facets must somehow be developed in concert with every other one. This task cannot be left to any one institution. Each institution is responsible for contributing to the development of the wholeness of each person in its charge.

Two simple but significant steps must be taken by any institution that conducts educational programs for adults: FIRST, it must recognize its responsibility for helping to promote the maturation process; SECOND, it must learn to relate and integrate its educational programs in order to assume effectively its share of this important task.

(e) *To provide, where needed, education for survival, in literacy, vocational skills, and health measures.* The education of adults should be an inclusive enterprise. Often programs of adult education increase during periods of economic prosperity. The affluent society becomes more concerned with so-called cultural affairs, when people have more time to spend in nonvocational pursuits, and when they have money to spend beyond what is needed to keep alive. Certainly the refinements of civilization can be of great importance, and the continuing education of adults in this area can be an important factor in the civilizing process.

However, large numbers of fellow human beings throughout the world are concerned, not with cultural or vocational refinements, but with the stark problem of survival. In many areas of the world, including parts of the United States, people either do not have the wherewithal to carry on above a submarginal level, or they do not know how to make the best use of what they have. In terms of importance and numbers of people served, one of the major goals of adult education is to help persons learn to develop and use skills basic to survival.

In many places today people are trying to exist on land that will not support them and by agricultural methods that would be inadequate even if the land were sufficient. A great percentage of the world's people can neither read nor write. And it is probably safe to estimate that most of the population of the world know little about elementary hygiene or health measures.

For the comfort and satisfaction of these deprived persons and for the safety of the rest of the world, it is paramount that these persons be helped. They must be helped, first, because it is the responsibility of those who have to share with those who do not have. Secondly, these adults must be taught how to read and write and how to do their work better, because the world today is too small to suffer sores on any part of its body without seriously affecting the other parts.

Some progress has been made in recognizing the extent and seriousness of this problem as well as in actually attacking it. But the surface has only been scratched. It is not just a question of pouring great sums of money into such an endeavor, but also of training personnel. This latter need has been almost ignored, so that few trained professional adult educators are involved in this widespread task of adult education.

Some work of quality has been accomplished by missionaries, foreign service personnel of various countries, and some personnel from the countries in which the programs are being conducted. But such an enormous undertaking needs to be attacked on a large scale by persons who are professionally trained to accomplish this task. No one group or nation should do this job alone or be expected to assume such an obligation. All kinds of groups, institutions and nations must work together to provide trained personnel and to attack this issue in which many of the world's serious problems originate.

2. A Structure for Adult Education

Adult education can be effective when structured through existing social institutions such as the family, the church, the labor union, the school, industry, and agricultural organizations. The word "institution" is used here to describe a corporate body whose members share some mutual concerns and functions expressed through some social organization.

If a task of adult education is to help us grow up, become more mature, and thereby live a more abundant life, we must be free to discover cooperative ways of accomplishing this, free from undue repression by private forces and by government. We must be free even to stumble and make mistakes and must recognize this as part of the problem of discovery and maturation. For this we need a social atmosphere conducive to the kind of growing human beings need to do in order to become truly human, in order to become the maturing persons we are capable of becoming. The institutions making up our society can provide this atmosphere.

Every institution in our society teaches its members something either formally through classes, lectures, meetings, and discussions, or informally through the policies and attitudes reflected in the organization. In the latter instance, the learning that takes place is usually incidental and is random learning through experience; but it is, nonetheless, learning. Unfortunately, in a number of our social institutions, this is about all the learning that takes place. They show little feeling of social responsibility and make little effort to carry on regular learning programs for the adult members of the institution.

Institutions sometimes see themselves as specialized organisms remotely associated with the whole of society, or associated in a way that would promote what they believe to be their own welfare. They often limit their responsibility for education to their specialization. Too few institutions assume a fair share of responsibility for those elements that compose a complete person. Many of us are so busy programming computers and thinking up ways to do things faster and more efficiently in order to reduce costs so we can make more money and buy more things, that we don't take time to find out either what's happening to us, or whether we need some of the things we are supposed to have, or whether the social order benefits or suffers by our activity.

Vast quantities of information about the adult exist. Our nature has been studied and reported by philosophers, prophets, writers of prose and poetry, and scientists for centuries upon centuries. We know much more about ourselves than we will take time and care to use. In most instances what we know psychologically and physically about an adult is directed toward training him to serve a specialized purpose. In a factory he is taught to run a particular kind of machine or tend a certain battery of switches and buttons; the military teaches him to do a better job of destruction than he could do without this training; the church teaches him to believe a certain way and sometimes to fortify his belief with the conviction that others who do not believe in the same way are lost.

If we are to grow up, the education of adults must be broad and diverse; every public or private institution in which an adult is involved must carry its share of this task. In every case the adult learner must have whatever he is learning integrated as much as possible with the whole of life. Each institution and learner will benefit from every other when we attempt, even in a small way, to try to help one another think through the whole problem of adult living. The alternative to this is fragmentation, which complicates human existence. When the church or the factory or the union or the farm group believes that it is its job to teach only a fraction of the picture, this group is failing society; it is failing because the learner rarely, if ever, has an opportunity to see the whole. He sees only the fragmented parts and no one has helped him to relate these parts. Consequently, we learners think as we have been trained to think —in a detached and incomplete manner. And such thinking can result in personal and corporate disaster.

Schools and colleges are as derelict in their duty to develop the whole person as are other institutions. Persons going from one course or subject to another see little relationship to their problems and life. They have been told that going to school and taking courses is good for them and that, after they are through, they will be educated. When finished, perhaps they can speak eloquently, or build bridges, or wrestle successfully with complex problems of logic; but they can also hate as intensively as their "unlearned" brethren, they can be as chauvinistic as those who have not had the good fortune to spend many years in formal learning, or they can have personal and family problems as others do.

One social institution after another either willingly or unknowingly contributes to immaturity by conducting narrowly designed programs of learning, by making decisions for us instead of teaching us how to make them, by using fear as a learning factor—all approaches that foster the process of fragmentation.

The most casual observer of human conduct can notice the results of too much control and fear, too much decision-making being done for us by others, too little participation, and too little understanding of freedom, discipline and restraint.

When we are disturbed, we seek some answer or release. Sometimes our struggles to find answers result in actions that only promote further immaturity. We may engage in physical and psychological violence, or we may become progressively less effective as citizens by trying to escape responsibility and doing nothing in order to keep out of trouble. We learn that it is easier to turn problems over to those who believe they know and to support their views, than it is to take our rightful place as contributors to the solution of problems.

The hate campaigns of today and times past have been nurtured by ignorance and distrust. Such social diseases as war, riots, and strikes are often the culmination of long neglected personal and group trifles. Leaders become enmeshed in personal power struggles and the real solutions to the underlying problems are never revealed. Ignorance and pride, the ever-present companions of force, are responsible for most social disasters, and force is at best a tentative solution to a problem.

Those of us who are responsible for the conduct of the affairs of our family and other institutions need to be taught to share, to participate productively, to use our emotions to promote maturation rather than destroy it, to recognize what we are doing, and to be able to evaluate our actions. These alternatives to force and hate and revenge need to be taught continuously by every one of the institutions in our culture with the patience and intelligent consideration necessary to effect learning.

Nor should it be assumed that only the underprivileged and the unschooled should participate in education of this sort. The privileged, the leaders, and the schooled need this kind of adult education as much as anyone.

We have to be taught to help ourselves and to use the opportunities extended to us. We have to be taught to be on the watch for any institution that purports to solve all our problems for us: for the politician who senses the obvious and gives people more and more while demanding less and less participation from them, except that participation required to keep him in office; for the labor union that avoids using methods requiring full participation of its membership; for the professional association concerned more with the welfare of its members than with that of the people it serves.

The solution to these problems, which are barriers to our personal and corporate development, is not a simple one; nor does the responsibility for causing them or solving them belong solely to certain persons or institutions. All persons and all institutions must do their part in this titanic struggle, not for physical survival alone, but for the survival and advancement of the human mind and spirit. Since we are all responsible in some way for causing the problem, we must identify and accept our share of the load of attempting to solve it.

We must first recognize our responsibility as individual parts of institutions that direct the way people are taught to think. Each of us belongs to at least one of these institutions and serves it in some capacity. Examples are the church, the family, industry, school, agricultural organization, government, hospital, library, service club, and union. All of these are adult educational institutions as well as whatever else they are. Each of these institutions causes some change in the way we think and act.

We are frequently disturbed because we think people just won't accept responsibility. They always wait for somebody to tell them what to do. Rather than complaining about this deficiency, we should develop a program of learning which would teach people how to assume responsibility, why they should assume it, and when, and where. We could help solve this problem by teaching each individual to handle as much responsibility as he is able and willing to accept.

Many persons have been told what to do all of their lives, in every institution in which they were involved. It is clearly

44

necessary for each generation to pass its knowledge on to the next, and much of this transfer must be done by showing and telling. Part of the knowledge to be transferred is how to think for ourselves and how to make a contribution that is uniquely ours. Here is where we sometimes fail. We fail to allow a person to share in the job of learning how to grow up. We try to do it for him, either because we want to be the boss and push somebody around, or because we love him so much, or because he's not smart or experienced enough yet. In any case we believe he's not ready to take on responsibility. Suddenly he is confronted with the problems of earning a living and caring for a family and the broad responsibilities of citizenship. Many persons have not been fortunate enough to have had instruction in these skills. Somehow or other these abilities are supposed to emerge full-flowered when a person becomes an adult, by which we usually mean when he has a big body and is twenty-one years old.

Learning how to live and to develop mature attitudes doesn't come about suddenly or mysteriously. It is taught somehow or other, or it is not learned at all. And, if it's not learned, then our reaction to life is to stumble along awkwardly or aggressively, to pretend we know, or to develop other defense mechanisms, many of which are wasteful and unnecessary.

The institutional approach can be a practical and effective way to solve many problems of adult education. It has striking advantages. We all belong to something; we gather together in these already established institutions. We have enough common interests to form a core for the operation of a program of adult education. Getting a group together in a particular institution is not only easier physically than trying to get a cross-sectional social group together, but it seems more natural to the participants. The potential learning group is already established in a broad sense. We do not have to set up completely new groupings.

45

Adults feel more comfortable in familiar surroundings, and such a feeling facilitates the learning process. Further, established institutions have existing channels of communication to be employed in developing and conducting programs of adult education. And institutions have a degree of continuity in both membership and administration that can be useful in maintaining stable educational projects.

Most existing institutions are convenient settings for developing and maintaining effective educational programs partly because such institutions have some kind of philosophy with which to start. Their goals may not be wholly desirable, but at least the members are used to thinking about goals, and the adult educator can start from there.

One striking disadvantage is that sometimes an institution teaches its members to become so absorbed in the institution and its views that they are partially isolated from the rest of society. Such teachings can weaken and eventually destroy the corporate body. But this disadvantage can be turned to an advantage. The adult educator can help this kind of institution gradually see the vital significance of assuming its total social obligation.

In the overall community approach to adult education each institution may send a representative to a general community meeting. Sometimes the result is that each representative holds to his institution's views to such an extent that a working degree of understanding is hard to come by. Most of us are not social-minded. We think we're giving up our rights when we compromise or expose ourselves to the views of others. However, a general community committee on adult education can be helpful. Such a committee, composed of representatives of the institutions constituting the community, can render a useful service by:

1. Disseminating and exchanging information about the different kinds of adult education programs offered in the community;

2. Promoting adult education throughout the general community and in the institutions making up the community;

3. Consulting with and assisting persons requesting help on adult programs.

Institutions should operate their own programs even if there is some duplication. Actually programs that seem to be duplicates are sometimes unique because what appears to be the same program may be handled in a different way by each group offering it. Of course, duplication can go to extremes, but so can standardization.

The fact that each institution has responsibility for its own programs should be emphasized. Sometimes cooperation with public agencies and other institutions can be advantageous. And the teaching in each institution should include some effort to relate that institution to the whole of society. This approach, plus the fact that many adult learners participate at some time or other in several institutions, can lessen the danger of parochialism.

One advantage of the institutional approach is that nearly every adult is part of more than one institution. For example, he has a family, works for some company, goes to a church, etc. This variety of institutions can help him see some social relationships, provided all the institutions to which he belongs help him see the broader view. Some institutions do not help in this matter. Those persons concerned with personal and social development should apprize such institutions of their responsibility to their members as well as to the community.

The institutional approach can spread the responsibility for the continuing education of adults throughout the entire fabric of society. Each institution will approach the problem in a different manner. These different approaches will help dispel the anxieties of those who fear conformity and will enliven and enrich the social scene. As larger numbers of institutions assume their share of responsibility for the education of adults, learning will be reinforced. When each institution puts some emphasis on adult learning, we members of the institutions can see more readily the importance of continuing education.

Every institution has a responsibility for teaching adults. This responsibility takes two forms: individual and social. Industries have a responsibility for helping their workers learn how to do their jobs better. They also have a responsibility of equal significance—to help their employees learn the relationship of the industry to the whole fabric of society. Religious institutions have similar adult education responsibilities. Each institution may have different subject matter or content to teach, but it has similar tasks: to help persons learn more about the particular institution, its purpose and beliefs, to help each individual exercise his own responsibility as a member, and to help each member understand how the particular institution relates to the social order of which it is a part.

We must have a real concern about what happens to people. Adult education should reflect this concern. People are not to be taught merely so they can be used or so certain institutions or groups can get more out of them. We should be taught to know more about ourselves and how to live an abundant life. We should be taught to know the satisfaction and value of giving our time, our talent, and our money to the enrichment of society through our family, our church, our vocation, and our community.

No one institution can do this task alone. At present some are shirking their duties in this field by reasoning that this is a job for someone else, so society suffers. Sooner or later we will have to learn to stop using each other and adult education, in a way which is good only for business or to promote some institutional scheme. It may take more disasters than we have yet witnessed before we realize that learning

48

is good for people and that people must be our first concern.

The idea of going to school is disagreeable to many adults. We are big people now, and we equate bigness with knowingness. Some adults believe that, since they've already been to school, there is no need to resume that experience. "School" calls up negative experiences in the minds of many of us, and we would prefer not to repeat them.

While some "school" atmosphere exists in all institutional programs of adult learning, it is often less noticeable in these organizations than in what we think of as "the school." Adults often feel more comfortable in programs held outside a regular school building since the setting is usually less formal. Then, too, it is socially advantageous to have more institutions share responsibility for the education of the adult.

There are, however, large numbers of people attending rather formal adult schools, and these schools are clearly serving a useful purpose in promoting the maturation and civilizing process. The public and private day and evening adult schools are thought of as educational institutions, while industries, churches, families, and unions are usually thought to exist mainly for other purposes. Yet these institutions, too, should become potent educational forces. All of them should assume a fair share of responsibility in this essential venture.

When more institutions take a responsible role in adult education, their contributions as corporate instrumentalities will help move the learners from an ego-centered to a more socio-centered life.

CHAPTER III

Some Specific Meanings of the Term "Adult Education"

To many persons adult education means "taking a course" or going to some kind of school, frequently in the evening. Many of us have been engaged in increasing our knowledge and improving our skills by attending schools of various kinds conducted by such institutions as industries, churches, unions, agricultural organizations, and hospitals. The educational work we pursue may range from something basic and elementary to something highly advanced and complex. All of this can be described more accurately as programs of education for adults or courses for adults. Great numbers of people attend Sunday school or classes for adults in religious institutions. This, too, is part of the wide area of learning called adult education. Colleges and universities offer special noncredit courses and lecture programs as addenda to what are considered their major teaching functions and these are referred to as adult education programs.

If we consider adult education as any kind of learning that alters the way we think about something, changes the way we behave, or adds to our supply of information and knowledge, then the programs mentioned above are only

51

part of the vast area included in the idea called adult education. A broader view of adult education must also include all the day-to-day exposure to life that every adult must experience if he is conscious. Listening to the radio, watching television, reading, talking to people, planting flowers, going to concerts, playing bridge or pool, and everything else an adult does is adult education of one kind or another.

Adult education can contribute to the civilizing process and the subsequent liberation of the human spirit and mind, or it can strengthen our tendency toward barbarism and help to forge stronger links in the chain of self-imposed and socially imposed slavery. Our inclination to classify and label everything and to feel uncomfortable unless everything is in a tidy categorical compartment has resulted in education's being thought of as "good." But, if adult education is inclusive, involving every organized or unorganized or disorganized experience we have, then adult education can be good or bad or indifferent depending upon our goals, the nature of the experiences we have, and the uses to which we put our experiences.

Although adult education can be any kind of learning experience systematically or randomly acquired, yet another meaning attaches to the term "adult education." This other facet of adult education is confined to the study and teaching of how adults learn and how they can be taught. The critical study of how adults obtain, interpret, and translate knowledge is included in this area of adult education.

We are, then, considering three major aspects of that area of education called adult education:

1. Adult Education as a Systematically Organized Program of Adult Learning:
    a. The School Type
    b. The Independent Study Type
    c. Participation Training Type;
2. Adult Education as Random Experiential Learning;
3. Adult Education as a Field of Study.

One of the basic tasks of the professional adult educator is to study the anatomy of adult education critically in order to determine its structural make-up and function. It seems helpful, therefore, to attempt to bring some meaning to the several terms called adult education by examining each of them in some detail.

The problem of communication besets all areas of inquiry. An analogy might be drawn between the fields of medicine and adult education. When we say "medicine," do we mean research in and study of the science and art of healing? Or the therapeutic tablets and liquids we take? We can mean either of these when we say, "Fred is taking medicine." The listener knows whether Fred is studying in a medical school or putting a spoonful of liquid in his mouth. Or *does* the listener know this? Interpretation depends to some extent on who is saying it, and on how, where, why, and when it is said. It also depends on the intelligence and emotional make-up of the receiver and the way he uses these learning factors at the time of instruction. In any case, interpretation is made easier when accurate, succinct definitions or descriptions are available and used.

The term "adult education" has different meanings, too, each of which is correct when used in the right place. The meanings of adult education are treated here in a little more detail than before.

1. Adult Education as a Systematically Organized Program of Adult Learning

(a) *The School Type.* Adult education is often mistakenly understood to mean only the kind of adult learning that takes place in classes led by teachers. This is an important facet of adult education, but only a part of the total area. Since a great part of this kind of adult education is conducted in schools of one kind or another, it is formal in the sense that it follows an established form or custom set by school-type learning. Such learning is usually directed by a teacher, who is expected to know the subject and is responsible for presenting the subject to the learner. The teacher lectures, asks questions, conducts discussions, gives examinations, may recommend that credits and certificates be granted, and, in general, is responsible for transferring information from various sources to the learner.

Any adult who ever attended school at all is acquainted with this type of learning. Adults sometimes stay away from this kind of adult learning program simply because they harbor unhappy memories of their childhood school days. However, many adults have either been able to cope satisfactorily with their childhood school traumas or the experiences were not as unhappy as they once seemed, since great numbers of adults regularly attend formalized learning programs. Statements are issued now and then indicating the number of adults attending such programs, but such pronouncements are estimates at best. Be that as it may, it is known that public schools, universities, colleges, unions, agricultural organizations, religious institutions, health organizations (e.g., Mental Health, March of Dimes, Red Cross), and industries are serving educationally tens of millions of adults throughout the civilized world. The large number of programs for adults in the United States, as well as in many other countries, staggers the imagination.

A program of adult learning characterized by a systematic, planned, and directed course of action is of necessity under the leadership of a teacher or leader who has some training and experience for the job he is doing. A relationship between the leader and the follower, the teacher and the learner, is established and maintained; it is often characterized by active participation by the leader or teacher and passive involvement of the learner.

Systematic programs of adult learning are not all conducted in schools of various kinds, nor do they all have the usual school-type, teacher-learner relationships.

54

A large number of participants pursue two other kinds of systematic learning activity. One is independent study and the other is participation training, a type of organized learning that uses a variety of procedures, and whose success involves a great degree of active participation among all persons involved in the learning experience: the group participant, the recorder, the resource person, the trainer, the observer, and the leader.*

(b) *The Independent Study Type.* Independent learning, which is more subject to control by the learner than by others, is important for adults. It not only helps the learner know more about the subject he is pursuing, but also helps him learn to discipline himself since he must largely direct himself in the learning adventure. Further, disciplined independent learning can ignite the spirit of inquiry and discovery which is the essence of real learning. Such activity helps the learner feel he can do things by himself. He can experience the thrill of independent discovery, which stimulates a desire for further learning.

Examples of independent systematic learning that put more responsibility on the learner than do the usual school-type programs are: correspondence courses, self-organized and self-directed reading programs, regular attendance at lectures and concerts with premeeting and postmeeting reading and study, self-teaching and study of hobbies, crafts, and languages.

Anything carried to extremes can be dangerous, even disastrous. Too much independence can make us unfit for life as social beings. Too little, however, can make us so overly dependent on others that we lose a part of that precious asset, our unique personhood. We are often con-

---

* The nature and the responsibilities of each of the participants are described in a book entitled *Adult Education Procedures,* by Bergevin, Morris, and Smith (New York: Seabury Press, 1963; paperback, 1966).

tent to let the other fellow do it; we shirk our personal responsibilities if someone else will take over for us. Many of us, therefore, find it difficult or impossible to carry on a productive, extended independent learning program with nobody to insist that it be done, to threaten or punish us. As a result we often fail to discover our real potential and are unable to offer to society the special contribution that can come only when each of us is a disciplined contributor.

(c) *Participation Training Type.* The other type of systematic learning, which does not follow the usual teacher-pupil-school pattern, is individual learning in a group context. The vital element in this educational activity is that every person in the program is trained to participate actively in the learning experience and so learns to assume some responsibility for its success. This process emphasizes the importance of learning a subject well and also puts great emphasis on what happens to the person while he is learning.

This kind of systematic learning is supported by the view that persons, not subjects, are being taught. Subjects are to be used for the participants and at least partly controlled by them. The participants are not forced into a predetermined pattern, often established by a small group of leaders or administrators who frequently orient the program toward administrative convenience rather than the students' needs.

The full-participation view of adult learning supports the idea that people should have something to say about some of the forces that shape them. Adults can be trained to use opportunities to determine together the content of their learning, the procedures to be used to accomplish it, and how teaching-learning personnel will be utilized. If we are to develop into mature persons who can take some responsibility for shaping our personal and social destiny, we should be trained to assume responsibility. Telling us that we must be responsible persons is not effective; we need to practice being responsible in the learning activity.

56

Responsibility and discipline and the direction of our potential into productive channels that promote maturation have to be experienced, not just talked about or wished for. Sooner or later we have to do something about all the "good" things we know about; but we have to be taught how to use the opportunities that we have. Some of us are better able than others to turn opportunity into reality. We can learn to help each other.

All of us can be helped to translate, interpret, and make more productive use of some of the ideas we have learned but know only academically. We need to be trained in how to learn, interpret, and translate into action what we have read and talked about. And we need training in how to help each other learn.

Systematic learning based on participation training* for *all* participants seeks to give each student a chance to learn about himself, his fellow learners, and the subject under consideration. It gives the learner an opportunity to explore, to feel free to say things without being laughed at or belittled. It offers the learner a chance to express his thoughts and feelings without necessarily having to please the teacher. One objective of this kind of systematic learning is to become a disciplined learner by being accepted and disciplined by your fellow learners and by helping to discipline your fellow learners. Adults trained to learn in this way know the importance of expressing their feelings and beliefs to their fellow learners, and they are expected to assume responsibility for what they say. Moreover, they learn to listen to others with the same understanding they expect to receive.

Systematic learning involving trained learners is designed to help us make the most of our learning potential by dealing with the nature of each learner, and by understanding how

---

* For a detailed treatment of this type of learning, see *Participation Training for Adult Education,* by Bergevin and McKinley (St. Louis: Bethany Press, 1965).

he tries to establish a relationship with his fellow learners and with the subject matter being treated. It rejects as faulty and anachronistic the view that only those who can learn through traditional procedures should be educated and that those who cannot should take up a trade. It further seeks to prevent learning from being prostituted as an expression of human vanity, or from being used by the privileged few to perpetuate the serfdom of the uneducated.

What can adults learn through a systematic program of learning based on the training of all the participants? Adults can learn how to learn; they can learn more about themselves, their fellow learners, and the all-important relationship they must establish and maintain with their fellow learners if maturation is to take place. Through understanding more about themselves and other learners and about why they feel and act as they do, adults can learn to express themselves freely and honestly and to listen to others do so. Adults can profit intellectually and emotionally from this experience. They can learn how to help one another by practicing helping one another during the group learning experience. Under these conditions, the subject matter can be learned to a greater profit.

Three types of systematic learning have been described: the school type, independent study type, and participation training type.

Systematic learning covers a broad area of adult education; consequently, it has a variety of characteristics:

1. The learner is an adult;
2. It can be pursued for credit or noncredit;
3. It is usually offered in institutions such as schools, colleges, universities, churches, factories, unions, agricultural associations, health organizations, and hospitals;
4. It may be vocational, cultural, spiritual, political, or physical;

58

5. It is planned and directed toward educational goals by a teacher or leader, or by the full cooperation and participation of all members of the learning team. It may also be self-directed;

6. It depends on the establishment and maintenance of a continuing educational relationship between those adults who teach and those who learn. This may be a teacher-student relationship in the traditional sense; or, when the adults have been trained to work together effectively as a learning team, each adult in the learning group may become to some extent both a teacher and a learner (participation training);

7. It may be a full-time or a part-time pursuit. (Most adult learning programs are part time.);

8. It may be voluntary or compulsory;

9. Systematic learning programs may offer certificates, diplomas, badges, ribbons, stars, etc. upon completion of the course, but sometimes the satisfaction of knowing is all the learner requires.

2. Adult Education as Random Experiential Learning

Random experiential learning takes place without planning or guidance and without an established purpose or goal. It just happens as we live. The acts involved in living, in doing what we have to do from day to day, contain a great variety of experiences from which we learn. Most of the time we are unaware of learning taking place. Learning is incidental to what we are doing in most instances of this kind.

We carry on our daily jobs—meeting people, solving problems, doing work. A kind of learning certainly takes place in these activities. For example, we may learn how to deal with people by trial and error through being exposed to people in social relationships. Or we may read a book, make a flower garden, or listen to the radio purely for pleasure, without any educational purpose or aim whatsoever. We learn something, nevertheless, from such random experiences. This kind of learning happens by casual exposure. It is not an organized program and learning is incidental to whatever our major purpose may be.

Random experiential learning is a big part of adult learning, and it happens continuously and unintentionally to all of us. We read for fun; we watch television as an escape, since the great bulk of it doesn't provide much else; we meet and talk with people; we pursue recreational activities; and we engage in community projects of all sorts. We learn something from all of this, but we do not engage in these pursuits in order to learn.

Random experiential adult learning can be identified by:

1. Absence of planning;
2. Lack of a learning goal or objective or purpose;
3. Being basically accidental in nature;
4. Taking place through everyday experiences other than those usually thought of as organized school or classroom learning experiences;
5. Lack of awareness on the part of the learner that learning is taking place at all;
6. The absence of a professional educator.

3. Adult Education as a Field of Study

Adult education as a professional field of study is systematically organized, but it is a body of knowledge and not a program. The major concerns of this discipline are to conduct research and to train professional adult educators, many of whom are granted academic degrees in this discipline. This field of study is directed toward: examining the nature of the adult as a learner; studying how to teach adults effectively; examining ways of translating, interpreting, and using available information obtained mainly from the behavioral sciences; seeking means of helping the adult learner discover, understand, and use personal and corporate resources in his struggle toward maturity; studying adult needs, wants, and expectations and the ways an effective interpretation and understanding of them can reduce fragmentation and bring about wholeness directed toward a productive life.

The professional field of study of adult education is not unconcerned about economics and vocational competence, but it is deeply concerned with helping the adult discover how to live a fruitful and satisfying life by balancing his vocational concerns with a variety of other activities which might include cultural, spiritual, recreational, and political pursuits as well as community service.

The professional field of study of adult education conceives of the growing and developing adult as a person seeking fulfillment and wholeness. It is concerned with the problem of what is needed educationally to put and keep us on the road toward our highest potential, toward becoming maturing citizens who contribute to the civilizing process. A vital concern of this discipline is to help us learn not just how to make a living, but how to live as completely as we can each day.

Adult education as a field of study examines critically adult needs in various environmental settings and the ways in which learning programs can promote a mature rationality in our lives and, through us, in the institutions in which we participate.

During the past twenty-five years programs for training professional adult educators have been receiving increasing attention in a number of American universities. Persons from many institutions in the American community, such as agricultural organizations, churches, libraries, hospitals, schools, mental health organizations, and other voluntary community groups, have found it beneficial to supplement their basic schooling with specialized training in conducting productive learning programs in their institutions.

A well-trained professional adult educator should know what to do with what he knows. He should be skilled in helping adults put the knowledge they have to work. He should also help learners obtain new information and better ways to use it.

Graduate instruction in adult education should be distinguished from some other areas of instruction in that it should emphasize both broad and specific training in the skills of relationship with others, in communication, and in social, philosophical, and historical concepts affecting human conduct. In addition to a thorough background of instruction intended to acquaint the graduate student with the human predicament, he should be trained in the skills of diagnosing, interpreting, and translating problems into practical situations that lend themselves to specific educational treatment. He should be trained to wed theory and practice into a program of adult learning directed toward effective behavioral change. A well-trained adult educator has had a solid background of psychological, sociological, and educational theory, which he has learned to interpret during a supervised field program of internship.

One objective of graduate adult education is to learn how to help every adult know more about what he is, what is expected of him, and what he can do. Graduate adult education must be established upon the philosophy that every adult can learn and can be helped to know more about what his mission in life is and how he can use his unique talents to fulfill it. Adult education is concerned with every adult: old or young, intelligent or dull, well or sick.

Adult education as a field of study is directed to: (a) the acquisition of knowledge through study, teaching, and research; (b) the dissemination of theoretical and practical knowledge through a professional training program.

Adult education as a profession has been emerging during the past two decades. Until recently, no thorough or extensive academic training was available in adult education, and people who practiced in that field came from a variety of other disciplines. Now persons are applying themselves to professional graduate study in this area.

An appropriate body of knowledge is gradually being assembled through an increasing amount of research directly related to the education of adults, and through the inclusion of related information in such fields as psychology, sociology, anthropology, physiology, and education.

Like all professions, adult education is evolving slowly. Some change can be discerned in attitudes toward the profession. An increasing number of persons are dedicating themselves to the professional study and practice of adult education.

The professional training of adult educators is usually carried on in university graduate schools and the adequately trained person earns a doctorate in this field.

CHAPTER IV

Some Major Problems in the Education of Adults

While examining the problems presented here, the reader should consider two points:

1. Careful preparation for adult education programs is of crucial significance. Successful learning requires precise diagnosis of the entire situation to determine needs, expectations of all concerned, abilities of learners, facilities and resources available, time needed, and time learners are willing to spend. Getting ready to learn and giving careful attention to what is happening to the adult learners during the learning program are important if productive learning is to be achieved.

2. The problems treated here are not exhaustive, but they represent and illustrate the kind of problems that should be explored.

A useful philosophy of adult education should relate the educational processes and procedures used to what we know about adults. When we try to examine the adult learner objectively, we discover a number of significant personal and social problems which we must consider and try to solve, or our efforts to educate will be unsuccessful.

Considering and clarifying current problems that inhibit or misdirect learning can be an important step in the diagnostic process in which we examine, analyze, identify, and evaluate the educational situation.

Time and energy are wasted by adult educators who plan and conduct programs of adult learning without considering the nature of the learner and, therefore, make little conscious effort to fit a program to that nature. Some adult education programs are based on immediate need, the crash-type program. Someone has an idea and can get some money and has the authority to persuade others to accept his views, so a program is established, designed to demand fast adjustments in the learner and supposed to result in immediate action. Another common program is the kind planned and conducted by persons who presume to know what is good for the adult. Sometimes they ignore the fact that change in behavior is a slow, laborious process, whose difficulties must be recognized and dealt with by *all* persons participating in the learning program.

People concerned only with training programs as distinguished from the long-term development of the learner through education, carry on the training program as if the process of training a person to sell merchandise, do a particular job in a factory, or think and act a certain way has little to do with behavior change. But this is a fallacy. Every adult educational or training exposure, whether it is mechanistic training or the longer developmental process, involves some change in the learner.

The more we can know about what we learners think and why we think and act as we do, the more likely we are to enjoy a satisfying and fruitful learning experience related to our nature. Many of the problems of adult education are not those of learning *per se*. We can learn to do many things that are not acceptable to society or that retard the maturation process in the adult learner. We have the task and responsibility of learning the "right" things, even if the "rightness" is only tentative, as it sometimes is. All human institutions must take a stand at some time. They must have some rules, beliefs, organization, and enough standardization to hold them together. When these institutions examine themselves to determine how they are doing in terms of their established goals, they may find it advisable to make changes. This process of evaluation, made necessary by change, is essential if an institution or an individual is to live abundantly in a world of change.

The adult can learn the so-called "right" things or the "wrong" things as these ideas relate to promoting the civilizing process or retarding it. Most concepts can be used for the wrong purpose, and the adult teaching-learning process has been no exception; consequently this important work needs a sound, constructive philosophical foundation. A sound foundation is based on honest struggling and seeking out of new ways to sense and further our responsibilities as co-workers in the civilizing process. This search can be made on the job, in the home, in the church, or in learning together about the great contributions literature, music, painting, and the social and physical sciences make toward our attempts to understand our nature and direct it in channels that promote the discovery of our civilizing potential and the emergence of a way of life that uses that resource.

The points that follow may help the reader identify some of the problems that complicate a philosophy of adult education and confuse the adult learner. In spite of complications arising in human existence whenever easy answers are not readily available, some activity still takes place. It is our task to determine, as well as we can, the nature of the activity and at least the tentative path it should take. Few answers fit all situations at all times. But we have to have some answers that work and will provide us with the support we need to seek and explore new avenues, new ideas, and new ways of carrying on. We have to have some place to stand while we look over the situation and develop a strategy for a new attack.

We might try to visualize our life as a running river and us as swimmers in the river moving downstream with the natural flow. We can't swim all the time. Now and then we must go ashore, rest and refresh ourselves, see where we've been, and decide where we're going. We have several choices we can make. We can drift along downstream as effortlessly as possible, exerting ourselves just enough to keep afloat or getting others to exert themselves in our behalf. Or we can swim upstream and become exhausted without having accomplished very much. Or we can move along with the stream, using our strength prudently to express a measure of independence while still floating with the inevitable and natural flow and movement of the stream itself. If we choose the last way, which seems appropriate for personal and social development, we will have selected a pattern that is natural but fraught with problems. When we work, struggle, and think in a moving, evolving, dynamic world, we often confront problems that seem to have no answer or so many solutions we can't select the right one. This is one source of perplexity that often confronts those of us who have decided to assume responsibility and share actively in the social drama. How can we select the right answer or at least the better one? These are questions adult education should help to answer or at least consider.

What should we adults know that may give us a broad enough base to help us in an intelligent and useful pursuit of happiness as "the highest good being a realization and perfect practice of virtue"? * We can't know it all to be sure, but we can strive to incorporate in our learning programs

---

* Aristotle, *Politics* (New York: Random House, The Modern Library, 1943), p. 293.

enough understanding of the problems besetting us so we can attack them intelligently and vigorously.

Indeed all of the problems are not treated here, but enough of them are exposed to help the careful observer become aware of their character and importance. The adult educator will have to identify these problems and deal with them, when he is establishing for his adult learning programs a philosophical base whose goal will give the endeavor meaning.

Here is a list of some areas that have something to do with determining how and what we learn and how we use what we learn. The way we deal with these points helps us establish a general philosophical orientation as well as a kind of emotional climate for learning. Unless such problems are considered and treated, constructive adult education can be difficult and unproductive. The problem areas are:

1. The Pursuit of Materialism;
2. The Fear of Ideals—The Desire to Be Practical;
3. All Men Are Created Equal;
4. Social Development and Pride;
5. The Marginal Citizen;
6. Teaching Subjects Rather than Persons;
7. Resistance to Change;
8. Formalized Education;
9. Originality and Conformity;
10. Attracting Adults to Learning Programs;
11. Learning to Live with Tentative Situations.

A thoughtful examination of these problem areas may be stimulated by the following brief descriptions of each area. A learning program could result that would not fill us with segregated and unrelated facts but instead might begin to help us adults see our world in relation to other worlds. Facts and information then become meaningful elements contributing to our struggle to learn to translate and interpret the vast, available reservoir of knowledge.

1. THE PURSUIT OF MATERIALISM

If religion has anything to do with faith and zeal, the present-day pursuit of happiness through the accumulation of things and our evident faith in materialism closely resembles a religious commitment. Twenty-three-hundred years ago Aristotle observed that "the avarice of mankind is insatiable." Today there is little reason to change this statement. Actually there are more opportunities for more people to be avaricious now than in the past. We have more money to buy more things, and the more we have the more we feel we need. We show each other the things we buy and talk about them with a reverence and respect usually associated with the deity. We feel temporarily alive and at our best when somebody admires a bauble we were fortunate enough to buy at an unusual place. If no more of these trinkets are available, we feel this situation warrants an even greater display of pride.

Our constant seeking for an answer to our existence, for our purpose in life, often leads us to surround ourselves with the protection of things. When we stop long enough to consider the degree of security we realize from these possessions, we see that it is slight, if it exists at all; but this does not deter us. We continue to hope that by possessing more than we need, by having things to show off to others, we may someday sit down among our things and answers will be revealed.

We accumulate for the sake of accumulating. We are restless and disturbed, and visible possessions sometimes give us a temporary sense of wholeness, of security. But, when this feeling of satisfaction begins to wear off, we need more and more and more. We need more money, larger homes, faster automobiles. Industry needs greater profits; labor needs a larger share of those profits in the form of wages; and government needs more money to give greater services.

Most advertisers do not help in this maelstrom of materialistic action. They tell us what we want by playing on the same old chords of avarice, greed, and envy—a trinity that helps mightily to further materialism.

Effects of this ideology can be seen in almost every human institution. Each must be bigger than anything anybody else has, or go faster, or make more noise. A kind of logic is employed to fabricate reasons to support this view. It is sometimes argued that this appetite for more and more is modern, a product of this fast-moving age. An excursion to the local library will reveal that this insatiable human characteristic was found in every age.

There is nothing new about materialism in its many subtle and overt forms. Neither is there anything new about the historical fact that over-emphasis and misuse of materialism and misunderstanding of its purpose have caused human distress and misery. Adult education must recognize this as a potential problem and help put materialism in its proper place by assisting us to develop a value system that nurtures the human creative spirit and puts people above buildings, computers, and administrative machinery.

2. THE FEAR OF IDEALS—THE DESIRE TO BE PRACTICAL

People sometimes say that principles or ideals are all right in theory, but people have to be practical; they can't spend all their time philosophizing about ideals; they have to program computers, make automobiles, sell groceries, and leave the fancy talk to those who have the time and stomach for it.

"Our job here is to make steel." This statement sounds solid and impressive. People are tough and know what they're doing. But it also sounds as if people are being used. And we are being used and fragmented by many of the institutions in our society. Most institutions behave as socially

71

isolated specialists. They have a particular job to do and any social coordination is largely up to the individual. A similar philosophy is pursued by many schools and colleges. Each department specializes in a particular subject, and the student integrates and coordinates, if he can.

It is not the business of a school, a corporation, a government, or a labor organization to look into the private lives of its citizens. But it is the job of each of these institutions to know enough about its total responsibility as a social entity, to see itself as part of a whole social pattern rather than an isolated profit-making or educational or service institution.

The "practical" person often functions as a partially unrelated fragment of the social whole. He minds his business and expects others to do the same. When enough of us think this way, we will exist in a society (which can hardly be called a society) of isolated parts, a society that promotes extreme individualism, divisiveness, and separatism, a society in trouble or moving in that direction because it is drifting toward an unnatural form of human association. People seek out some kinds of association for protection and psychological security. We naturally want and need one another even if we act otherwise at times.

When each institution expects others to provide the essential social integrating force, we are fast approaching an anarchical situation that is socially disastrous. When parents expect the school, the church, and the government to take care of their children, maintain standards, and do the teaching the parents should do, we are in grave danger.

Each of us and each institution of which we are a part can improve society if we become involved in thinking about principles, about social standards, about ideals. Institutional and personal ideals should include some direction toward social responsibility and relationship.

Institutions often try to meet their social responsibilities by suggesting that their employees get into outside organizations such as service clubs, the scout movement, and churches—the kinds of groups that handle that business. Besides, it's good public relations. But the ideals have to work on the inside as well as the outside of our institutions. We should not have two separated groups: one that deals exclusively with the problems of the workaday world and the other that limits itself to the problems of personal maturation and the civilizing process. We won't function well in this divided manner. We grow or deteriorate everywhere not just in the Y.M.C.A. or in church. If ideals are needed anywhere, they are needed everywhere. Nothing can be more practical in the long run than the establishment of ideals, and the practice of social and personal responsibilities based on those ideals, by all institutions composing the social fabric.

3. All Men Are Created Equal

Confusion and irresponsible behavior result from misinterpreting the meaning of equality.

In a society that promotes the dignity of the individual it is of paramount importance that each person be considered equal before God and the law, that each of us sees justice done regardless of our position in society. This is an ideal worth struggling for. Like many ideals it is one we have not completely realized. Privilege too often dictates what will happen to people. People without money or position still languish in jail or get short shrift in some hospitals. Charity and justice are often related to who we are rather than the fact that we are human beings. The struggle for human dignity has nonetheless produced some hopeful results.

It is decent and appropriate that every one of us be considered equal to every other person as fellow human beings seeking satisfaction and happiness from life through justice and the extension of opportunity. To think of us, however, as equal in all respects because we are equal in some is nonsense. That we are of different capabilities, temperament, and size goes without saying. We have often misunderstood or abused the idea of equality. We sometimes cry loudly about our rights without thinking of equating our rights with our responsibilities. We can gain and maintain our rights and privileges by exercising our responsibilities as citizens.

No one can demand as a right that society owes him a free living if he is able to work and is extended the opportunity to work. No able person can justly expect more from his government than he is willing to give because he is equal in some respects and has rights and privileges. When a democracy functions properly, the government is of about the same quality as the people it serves. We all have the right and the responsibility to express our considered judgment and talent as free citizens and to make certain demands on society for our personal and corporate welfare. At the same time we must balance our expectations from society by giving our own time and talent and money to the corporate cause.

Our understanding of equality and of our rights and privileges can be clarified in some programs of adult education. But these concepts cannot be merely memorized and talked about. They have to be taught by demonstration, by providing opportunities, and by showing us how to use the opportunities provided. These ideas, like many that confuse us, must be taught through many institutions, not just in a "school." They must be learned by having experiences that can help us under patient, intelligent direction. By such learning we can use our influence to preserve and promote human dignity through an important kind of equality.

4. Social Development and Pride

We are born self-centered creatures. Our immediate concern is for our own welfare alone. We know little or nothing of others, of their needs and feelings, except as the needs and feelings of others are associated with the services we demand. As we become older, we are gradually acclimated to a social milieu. We learn to deal with the feelings and needs of others in order to get what we need or believe we need. So we make adjustments, but we make many of these adjustments not to help others, but to find ways to get around others in order to accomplish our personal ends. Some of us experience an arrested social development at this stage and never get beyond trying, by one means or another, to get what we want with little or no regard for the social consequences.

We hear this type of arrested social development expressed when people say, "You'd better get what you can while the getting is good. Nobody will look out for you if you don't look out for yourself. If the other fellow loses out, that's his hard luck. Society is like a tank full of sharks; you've got to protect yourself."

Often the young child finds he can get what he wants by using fang and claw; and, if his experiments are uninterrupted by competent guidance, there is little change as he grows older in his way of serving self, except perhaps in the use of more subtle and elusive means.

The chronological age at which social development may stop can vary widely. Persons at forty-five may understand their fellow men no better than persons of ten or twelve. It is, therefore, of great significance to survival that the continuing education of adults be considered as important as that of children. Adults exert the power, set the standards

75

and, in truth, determine the direction of society. Adults who make social and institutional decisions at a twelve-year-old emotional and intellectual level are establishing patterns for the next generation to carry on at that level.

Since we have assumed that the preservation and advancement of society depend on our learning how to live together, we will have to assume further that we must also develop more effective ways to learn how to live together.

The problem of teaching us to become civilized is complicated, and we should recognize from daily happenings in our society that we have a hard struggle ahead and a long way to go. It becomes quite involved because only a few things are taught to us in common. For example, most of us are taught that we should keep out of trouble, respect and follow certain religious ideas, and be patriotic. But wide differences exist in individual families and groups. Persons are taught by principle and example within the family circle and by groups with which they are associated. Sometimes the customs followed and the beliefs taught differ widely. Some of this teaching confuses and separates the human family by teaching, through one device or another, the unquestioned superiority of one group of persons or one set of ideas over any other.

Well-meaning parents sometimes teach children distrust and fear and hate; and social institutions sometimes confuse adults by making declarations that cannot be reconciled with their actions. In addition each of us is a unique being. The result is a complex personal and corporate situation.

As children we begin to learn to be social beings. Our parents, playmates, schools, and churches all work on us. Sometimes these teaching agents are at odds with one another, adding further confusion to the already complicated state. We grow up in this environment, or at least we become older and get bigger physically. We are then dubbed adults.

The problems of learning not only persist but increase in

complexity because as adults we sometimes think we know more than we do. We believe that being adult of itself increases our knowledge. This is partly true, but we are often unable to do much with the added information we have because we still try to use it as we learned to do as children. The problem of helping us participate intelligently and reasonably in our social order as adults while we still operate partly as children, is momentous. As candidates for adult education, all of us are products of the training of our youth.

We still feel we must keep our toys to ourselves, and we demonstrate this by failing to give of ourselves to others. Part of our "natural" ego-centered tendency probably has been taught to us. If we are born with a tendency toward self-centeredness, we have accentuated this characteristic by what we teach one another.

Self-centeredness is not a quality we can completely eliminate; rather it is a characteristic we will have to learn to control and live with. Self-esteem, the respect one needs to have for himself as a human being, is not synonymous with self-centeredness. When we see ourselves as the center of everything, when all we really want to know and to care about is ourselves and how life can be regulated to suit us, we are unfit to assume our responsibilities as adults.

One of the great problems of adult education is to understand ourselves as self-centered creatures struggling toward social-centeredness. The problem is complicated by the support self-centeredness gets from its ally, pride. Pride and self-centeredness cause great difficulty in adult education directed toward the civilizing process. They stand in opposition to our growth as social beings.

It is difficult, if not impossible, to unlearn anything completely. We can by education relegate certain undesirable habits and traits to a secondary position, but they are probably still around in the recesses of our thinking and could come up again to plague us. We've been taught to be

77

proud about one thing or another, and this pride fits into our self-centered nature and fortifies us against learning to love one another and learning to see ourselves as important units of a larger whole. Our parents are proud of those of us who are smarter than others. We're proud of our old school and demand that it beat all comers on the athletic field to such an extent that school athletics have often taken on professional characteristics. We take "justifiable pride" in many things. We strut about wearing badges, uniforms, and gowns; we struggle for recognition so people will look upon us as better than they are or at least better than somebody else.

Each day in almost every institution we are subtly taught the importance of personal and corporate pride if we want to be somebody. On the other hand with much less conviction we are taught a few clichés about the destructive nature of pride.

Pride and self-esteem are two different things. We don't have to precede the word self-esteem with "justifiable" as we do the word pride when we want to make pride sound respectable. We need to learn that these are two quite different terms and use them correctly.

Self-esteem is vital to our psychological health. It is that trait that gives us a proper perspective on ourselves and our fellow human beings. It helps us identify ourselves and respect ourselves for what we are and can become. But inordinate self-esteem becomes pride, a destructive element.

Here again we are trained to be confused. What shall we do? Make an honest effort to understand and respect ourselves and our need to relate to others? Or be tops in humility?

How and what we think about this problem of personal and social growth is important. Remember that we are concerned about adult education and how it relates to growth in all areas—in chemistry or art or social problems.

78

We are not discussing just certain kinds of learning programs with a philosophical or religious or sociological orientation. We are considering *any* kind of constructive adult learning. An adult who knows something about himself and his need to develop as a social being as well as an individual, becomes a better learner, a better worker, a better citizen, a better person. The industrialist, labor unionist, agriculturalist, or school instructor who believes the learner must get that "social stuff" someplace else is selling himself and the learner short. He is choosing a narrow path, which will lead inevitably to conflict and further confusion for himself and the learner.

5. THE MARGINAL CITIZEN

A marginal citizen is a person who is unable and/or unwilling to carry what his society considers his fair share of the social load over an extended period of time.

Marginality is a matter of degree. As in emotional health, none of us is completely healthy. Our disorders may range from an occasional feeling of discomfort to a need for constant attention or even incarceration. We are each somewhere in a continuous sequence; most of us are slightly to moderately marginal; some of us are severely so. It is a problem of the human family in which we all share.

While adult education deals with all citizens, this particular discussion about the marginal person involves a limited but very important number of people who need more specialized educational treatment. Actually, submarginal would probably be a more accurate term, but it has undesirable psychological overtones. To be technically correct, everybody is marginal in some area of adequacy related to citizenship; but, in order to identify this problem more clearly, the term marginal as used here will refer to those persons least able to carry out their social responsibilities.

A good citizen is identified as a good person who takes an

active and constructive role in the society of which he is a part. Clearly, this use of "citizen" is much broader and more inclusive than the way we usually use the term. We often associate the word "citizen" with a person who owes allegiance to a particular government and has certain rights and privileges related to this association. Further, a good citizen is often erroneously thought to be a person who merely behaves himself and votes on election day.

But citizenship in a democratic society must mean more. The good citizen in a democratic social order is one who participates actively and constructively in many of the social institutions that make up the fabric of that society. He is aware of his responsibilities, rights, and privileges and exercises them. He must also be what Aristotle would call a "good person" in that he strives to attain a high standard of values, which he makes felt in the institutions in which he actively participates. This kind of good citizen, who is also a good person, does not blindly follow others when such activity means betraying principles that would creatively release human kind.

Ideals are difficult to achieve. Since we are all somewhat marginal for one reason or another, we do not understand or discharge our responsibilities of citizenship as well as we might. But most of us are able to function with some degree of efficiency and make some contribution toward advancing the civilizing process. For a variety of reasons some persons do not contribute as much as they take. These persons might be characterized as marginal citizens. We must try harder to correct this problem of marginality, or the social order we envisage may be impossible to realize. Each social order is limited by the size of burden it can carry.

Since the dawn of conscience people have been aware of the problem of the person who seems to be inadequately fitted to live as society would like him to live. This person, who is not able to make a go of it in his environment, may

80

be alcoholic or always in trouble or unable to read or write or unable to hold a job or plagued by organic or functional illness; he may not adjust well to the misfortunes he meets in his life and so become emotionally ill; or he may have a congenital mental or physical defect, which places him out of competition in society, or be one of the aged who have placed more limitations on themselves than nature has. Further, marginal citizens can be found among persons who do not have to work because they have sufficient financial support to live without working. They fritter away time and energy in pursuits that contribute little or nothing to their personal maturity or the betterment of the social order.

As it is today, so it has been throughout recorded history: the development of sensitivity toward human need by other humans has been a slow and painful process. The teacher, the physician, and the priest came into being as specialists concerned with human need, and each attempts to provide part of the answer to the problem of building a civilized society.

With the development of urban dwelling, cooperation among persons in groups reached an ever higher level. The achievement of learning to live together and help one another appears to have been based primarily on the survival needs of the populace rather than on the more mature concept of helping another person merely because the person needed help. To offer help because a person needs help with the helper expecting no credit or personal gain of any kind is a stage of maturation which was not reached by the ancients and is for the most part still strange in the present evolutionary stage of civilization. A more pragmatic approach used in the past, and still used, is the idea that society must learn to cooperate in order to preserve itself, and that something must be done about the social mavericks in order to maintain a social structure.

The life of Egypt for 3,000 years was inextricably associated with religion. Three major concerns dominated Egyptian thought for nearly thirty centuries: eternal life, order, and harmony. These views, carried on for such a long period of time, undoubtedly had a profound effect on the attitudes of the people. The seeming timelessness of their architecture and their traditions provide constant evidence of the place in their society these concepts held.

Professor Breasted* informs us that about 4,000 years ago during the period of Egyptian history called the Old Kingdom traces of the idea of "future accountability" appeared, and the concept was fully developed about a thousand years later in the Middle Kingdom. This idea indicated that, "the future destiny of the dead must be dependent entirely upon the ethical quality of the earthly life." People became concerned about giving "bread to the hungry, water to the thirsty, clothing to the naked, and shelter to the shelterless." The reason for this social concern was to store up treasures in heaven, a hope of personal reward in the future life, rather than to help people because they needed help. This notion is not unrelated to our present reward-punishment concept. Nevertheless, people were beginning to think about their responsibility for one another and the way they related to each other.

Our attitude toward the marginal citizen is colored by our society's view of several basic problems related to the nature of man and our interpretations of this basic concept. Religions have always played an active and powerful role in moulding the views that determine the fundamentals of social outlook in any era. The evolution of the kind of civilization in the Near Eastern and European cultures furthered the view that every person was a child of God, implying an equality of personhood whose potential might elevate those less fortunate in health, wealth, or intellectual

---

* James Henry Breasted, *A History of Egypt* (New York: Charles Scribner's Sons, 1909), pp. 173-174.

capacity to a position of spiritual and social dignity. Another significant view emphasized the responsibility of one person for another. These are two colossal ideas, and to a limited extent they form the base on which our present-day social order operates.

Obviously a few samples from the long history of human relationships will do little more than show us that our kind has been concerned to some degree with more than self for many centuries. A socio-centered view of person toward person did not spring forth as a principle of civilized society in one leap. Casual observation indicates present society has a long way to go to reach the kind of healing reality expressed so eloquently by Erich Fromm in *The Art of Loving** when he points out that we can love one another because we *are*, not because we "behave" or are beautiful or admirable or for any other reason.

For centuries, some people have thought of trying to become a human family. To have some feelings of personal selfishness is only human. It is a big job for humanity to counteract its natural behavior, but part of humanity has been bravely and fairly consistently tackling the job for years and some progress can be observed.

We change slowly, *but we can change*. This fact should be the cornerstone of the attack. Revolutionary changes usually result in revolutionary reactions, and the net gain is often negligible. Change based on thoughtful preparation and positive, consistent action supported by a knowledge of our tradition and our nature will survive and become a creditable part of our tradition.

Much valuable energy goes to satisfy our urge to do something now and then, preferably something "good." This often serves more as a relief to our pent-up tensions than as a solution to our social problems. The problems of people on

---

* Erich Fromm, *The Art of Loving* (New York: Bantam Books, 1963), pp. 33-35.

the margin of society are not playthings or opportunities to provide an occasional personal or mass psychological release. They are serious problems that demand consistent thought and action, the best we can achieve. Action carried out without considering the factors in each case often results in retrogression. It is not hard to get the ear of large and influential groups of people when we can appeal passionately to them to right wrongs and slay social dragons. This approach is well known in some political, religious, and educational circles. We seem to follow some kind of Pied Piper regardless of the amount or kind of schooling we have had. The more schooled talk longer and use a few large words to tell the same story.

Too often we aggravate the issue by using quick remedies and ill-considered emotional approaches based on sympathy rather than understanding. Persons who are dependent sometimes become more dependent. This happens because we try to solve their immediate problems without conducting a program of help, including appropriate adult education, which would train them to help themselves when possible and to help themselves by helping others.

The idea of helping those on the social margin must be freed from sentiment and selfishness and looked upon as essential to fulfill our obligations as trustees of the civilizing process. It is vital to lasting progress that we consider carefully how we go about fulfilling our obligations to others needing our help. In this problem the means are inextricably related to the end.

To deal with the problems of those of us who are what might be called marginal, we need an attitude that will help us carry on to a more lasting and satisfying solution. We cannot begin by considering the problem a nuisance. Neither should we approach the problem from the standpoint that it is for the advantage of the more fortunate that the unfortunate must be assisted.

There are several approaches to minimizing the problem of the marginal person and helping him advance toward social maturity. These approaches include:

1. Eliminating persons considered marginal;
2. Ignoring persons considered marginal as much as possible;
3. Helping these persons because it is necessary in order to preserve society;
4. Helping them because they need help.

The fourth suggestion in this list indicates a degree of understanding and maturity we have not yet reached. We rarely give or help *for no other reason* than that the situation or person needs what we have to give. Usually we are motivated by ego-centered forces characterized by what is expedient. Since we are inclined to take the short-term view, our attitude toward a problem of such magnitude as the marginal citizen reflects our opportune-based position. When we are more concerned with our relationship to authority and advantages we might gain than we are with our relationship to what we believe is right, we can do no more than skim the surface of the job to be done. We become ensnarled in a progressive morbidity distinguished by over-emphasis on vocational and social advantages which may accrue to us. As we become more civilized, our work in helping one another out of this human dilemma will be reflected in a wide social concern.

Most of us, who are slightly or moderately marginal are able to contribute as much as or more than we take. A serious threat to a social order comes from those of us who are less fortunate and are seriously marginal. Those of us who can not read or write, who are in prison, who are constantly out of work and are regular recipients of welfare, who are in mental hospitals, who are alcoholics, are persons who are in trouble or sick or dependent on society and need help. Many of these persons can be helped by trained adult educators who can intelligently apply the best in adult education.

With proper continuing education, many marginal citizens can be helped to carry a share of the social load, even if it is a very small share. Everybody can do something, and the greatness or smallness of the contribution is not as important in this instance as the fact that each of us is continuing to learn how to share, how to play his part. It is equally important that each of us learns that we have a part to play, that we are needed.

Some of us probably will have to be taken care of no matter how much effort is expended in our rehabilitation; but this dependent group can be reduced to a small number of persons. Most adults will respond to persistent and appropriate teaching—*even those who appear hopeless.*

A problem as serious as educating the severely marginal citizen cannot be lightly treated. The fruits of a free society should be shared by everyone, but everyone needs to contribute if we are to enjoy the potential of this kind of living together. Some of us don't know how to contribute; some of us don't have a chance; others can't do much—we are sick or too old or incapable; and some of us aren't interested. Every one of these reasons has to be examined and treated.

It is difficult to know exactly how many persons would be considered so marginal that they would be real or potential social liabilities, but we have approximate figures that are sufficiently accurate to reveal lucidly the need for action. In one state of less than five million persons, about 600,000 people fell into the area of marginality requiring serious attention. This represents more than ten percent of the population. These persons were in the following categories: about 300,000 functional illiterates; 100,000 to 125,000 alcoholics; 71,000 welfare recipients; 10,500 in state prisons; and 16,000 in hospitals for the mentally retarded and the mentally ill. These figures were taken in Indiana in 1963, during a prosperous economic period.

The attitude of persons concerned with this problem and its solution is most important. Money and facilities are needed, but our concern for people, and the way we attack the problem are of far greater significance. While this view is not present-day currency, it will reappear when we have had time to evaluate the lasting results of the speed-money-facility concept, which has enveloped a wealthy, nervous, and uncertain society.

CHAPTER V

Some Major Problems in the Education of Adults (continued)

6. TEACHING SUBJECTS RATHER THAN PERSONS

A traditional teaching-learning pattern has been followed without much change since antiquity. A person who knows tells or shows one who doesn't know. If the learner is smart, it may not take long to teach him; if he is not so smart, the job may have to be repeated. With this idea the learner is "used" to learn the subject. He is a vessel into which certain information is transferred.

All sorts of procedures have been used to stimulate learning. In some countries a thief was taught not to steal by cutting off his hand. People who questioned the social order were taught to respect their "betters" by having their livelihood taken away. Fear has always been used to stimulate learning. Fear of physical punishment has been a long-time associate of the teaching-learning process.

Little consideration was given the learner beyond making sure he could absorb a certain amount of information and react to it. What the learner learned about life, the life about him as well as his own life, was something he picked up as well as he could as he went along.

In later years when learning became more formalized in schools and was made more generally available, the kind of learning that might help a person to understand relationships, to see himself as a maturing part of the social whole, was relegated to extracurricular activity. Sometimes a few formal courses in civics and history were supposed to accomplish this task. Generally, the job of integrating the various ideas and facts was not done at all. The person had this task to do himself; today, for the most part, he still has this job to do.

We need to be taught to think in an organized way, to make discreet choices, and to make the best use of what we have for ourselves and for society. This premise is generally acceptable to everyone, but few of us do anything about it. We usually operate on the fallacious assumption that, if we teach enough subjects to both adults and children, they will learn what they need to fit into a productive vocational and social environment; we consider the traditional subject approach the primrose path to learning. But, if we study and observe at all, we know that teaching subjects does not necessarily make educated people.

We don't know much about who we are or what we can or should do, and we prove our lack of knowledge by getting into difficulties with ourselves, our families, and our national and international associates. The best adult learning or teaching we know will probably not solve all our problems and make us perfect beings, but we already know a great deal we are not using.

In successful adult education the learner must be thought of as a unique person, capable of some kind of learning. These are foremost ideas. To bring about desirable change in the adult learner an educational program must be oriented to the learner. Significant and fundamental adjustments and changes must take place in the programs of education for adults. Not only must there be more and greater variety of programs with more people involved; but the programs must be suited to the persons who are in them, to their natures and needs.

Programs of adult education are usually subject oriented and mechanistic. The programs often fit the administrator's pattern better than they do the learner's need. Too many adult education programs have been built around an administrator's knowledge of the usual school or college program. Buildings, money, and management personnel overshadow the learner, who in reality is the only purpose for the program at all. Most planning talk will center around how to get money, rooms, and teachers and what kind of subjects should be taught. One administrator said he didn't have time to study the needs of the learner or the community and the position his institution could fill in satisfying those needs. He pointed out that time was important and they had to get started right away, that studying the community and the potential learners would delay things.

Persons have too often been thought of as something to put into various categories like interchangeable machine parts. The significant danger is that more of this mechanistic thinking and action is likely, since every day there are more and more people with whom something has to be done. Neither are people scattered about anymore. They are pressed together in fast-growing metropolitan centers. In the minds of some this makes categorizing and numbering people more necessary in order to operate the social order efficiently.

On the surface it seems less troublesome to place learners in subject areas that fit a traditional educational pattern than to study the adult educational problem carefully. It appears easier to fit people to subjects than to take time to discover what is needed, why it is needed, and how the learner can relate to what is needed. It takes skill to accomplish this kind of diagnosis—skill and a larger degree of professional competence than many persons responsible for adult education programs possess.

The learner must be treated as a person. He must be regarded as the reason for the learning program. His experience and ability must be discovered and utilized in planning and conducting the kind of learning program that fits his nature as a learner and satisfies his needs. Subjects and resources are vital. They are as fundamental as medicines are to the sick, and just about as useless and potentially dangerous in the hands of those who don't know what is wrong with the patient or how to find out what's wrong.

We shall have taken an important step forward when we learn to use subjects so they satisfy the discovered needs of adult learners.

7. RESISTANCE TO CHANGE

Our desire to be secure and to keep things as they are in a changing, moving, developing world often creates ambivalence within us. This characteristic is not reserved for certain kinds of people but exists in all persons. Everyone tries to find some kind of security. Some of us surround ourselves with things: gadgets, furniture, clothes. In many persons' minds money is the prime source of security. Things and money may help to establish a feeling of security, but the amount needed for this feeling seems undetermined.

Some psychological and materialistic security appears necessary for the full development of the human personality, but sometimes this security becomes our most important objective. Time and again conversation deals with how much retirement money a person will get, how soon he can retire, how much vacation he gets. Here again a task of adult education comes to the front. How can we learn to make intelligent choices, to exercise discreet judgments? How much is too much? What are the true values of work and leisure in our lives?

92

When does a concern about our security—our financial welfare, our health, the things we own—become a perversion? Our over-concern appears to be related to our tendency to resist change, to want things to stay as they are or were. We seem to think we will feel more secure in a changeless situation. While such resistance appears in us at all ages, it usually becomes more pronounced as we grow older. Older persons generally see less opportunity and time to get the things they feel they need; consequently they think they must hold to what they have.

Unless the adult educator is aware of this resistance, much time will be wasted. We resist change and seek security because we are trained to think in these patterns. As a rule we are not trained to think in developmental, flexible terms. We are bound to the familiar; we like to sit in the same chairs, to eat the same food, to go to the same places, to think the same thoughts. Our thought patterns can become stereotyped. "I've been doing this (or that) all my life, and it's too late to change now." As persons grow older, they tend nostalgically to see the wisdom of grandfather's ways and slowly get ready to die—first mentally, then physically. Adult education must deal with these psychological and physiological problems of aging.

Resistance to change is natural, but so is the will to combat this resistance and seek change. We know people can learn at any age and many do. The unfounded notion, "I'm too old to learn," has caused many adults to shun their responsibilities as active citizens and has lost to society the experience and talents of many of its most experienced members.

Nearly every adult can change the way he thinks if he wants to and follows the desire with action. Change can take place in any living human being. This includes normal adults and those who are emotionally and mentally disturbed. The human body and its thinking apparatus are marvelously resilient structures.

The question is clearly not whether we can change, but whether we will take the time and make the effort necessary to study our nature and find how to fit that nature appropriately into a changing, moving, developing environment.

That resistance to change can be overcome was clearly demonstrated by the author in a long-term project of adult education among persons who were mentally ill and living in a mental hospital. Obvious changes in the way some of these persons reacted to learning problems and to one another took place during the extended experiment. Some groups were composed of moderately ill persons and they generally made faster progress. Other groups were composed of persons who were severely ill. Even those persons who had become seriously deteriorated responded to carefully conducted and appropriate learning activities, some of which helped after a time to bring about identifiable changes in attitude and behavior.

All of us can improve or change, whether we are thirty or seventy years of age. There are, to be sure, certain physiological and psychological differences in the various adult age groups. These differences must be known and dealt with in each of the learning programs conducted. The adult educator must know the participants and study their needs, capabilities, and willingness to learn, much as a physician must get to know his patients and skillfully diagnose their complaints. The competent physician uses different therapies for treating different diseases and treats most of them successfully. So it must be with the adult educator. He must know what a person seventy years old is like, how he learns, why he behaves as he does, and he must proceed accordingly. The same will hold for those thirty. The same medicine cannot be used for all diseases, nor can the same approaches to learning be used for all persons. But all persons can learn if they are intelligently and skillfully helped.

As we continue this discussion of some of the problems

94

confronting the adult educator, it should become increasingly clear that a function of the professional adult educator is to get to know the learner and proficiently arrange situations that will make learning possible. Again a parallel can be drawn between the work of the adult educator and the physician. The physician does not heal. He discovers the need of the patient; then he tries to establish a situation with chemical or mechanical or psychological aids to assist nature to take over the healing task, to re-establish a kind of balance, a homeostasis. He doesn't "heal" a patient any more than an adult educator "learns" a student.

So the adult educator must be acquainted with the learner and with the learning equipment—the subjects, procedures, and physical needs. He must then bring the learner into a meaningful relationship with what is to be learned and allow learning and the changes of attitudes and behaviors that learning can bring about to take place. We can get more productive results in this constant renewing process if we can learn to use some of the old values with the new.

We need to be active, to be prepared for, and to make appropriate changes and adjustments. Although we tend to resist change, often to our disadvantage in a changing world, we are not to assume that this is the way we are and that nothing can be done about it. We are able to grow and develop throughout our entire lifetime.

We should change not for the sake of change alone, but rather when such adjustments help to keep us in the mainstream of life. We can learn to base change on what will help us identify and use our greatest mental and physical potential.

8. Formalized Education

Formal education is a conventional method of promoting learning, usually characterized by a planned, systematic program conducted in a schoolroom, that bases most learning on the experiences of the learner in the classroom. It can sometimes be identified by a rigid atmosphere caused partly by lack of full learner participation, a set pattern of courses, a time limit, and teaching procedures that set the teacher and learner apart.

Our system of education for adults and children confuses many persons instead of helping liberate them. Time, energy, and money are spent in conducting programs of courses integrated faintly or not at all. Too often we come out the same door we went in. There is inconclusive evidence that more courses of the kind presently offered will truly liberate people and help them mature. Even courses unrelated or remotely related to our needs keep us temporarily out of mischief, but many of them do not contribute enough to helping us learn to improve our ability to examine our value system, to make discreet choices, or to become active participants in advancing the civilizing process.

The adult learner is a product of all his experiences, including the educational ones. The adult educator gets the adult who has been schooled by the traditional system. And the adult student expects what he always got from school— a certain amount of information given in a certain time, mostly by lecture. Getting an adult who has been trained to view learning as a fragmented series of experiences that start and end between the covers of a book to understand the need for life-long learning, is a challenging problem of adult education.

In most kinds of educational programs, formal or not, we have great difficulty relating the "book-learning" aspects of education to the functional. Such a relationship is often neglected in traditional, formal programs. In areas of pure research the relationship between theory and practice may be remote and not of great concern; but very few adults are in this area of learning or in areas where dealing with abstract concepts can eventually make substantial contributions to human advancement. Yet this unrelated approach to learning is used frequently in all institutions involved in adult education, probably because those in charge of the learning programs are emulating what they have seen and been taught. The idea is to get a book, have the adult read it, tell him what he read, see whether he can tell you what he read, and let it go at that.

While we clearly need nonfunctional or abstract learning in all kinds of adult education, the point at issue here is that there has been too little emphasis on the kind of adult education that can help the learner see meaning in terms of his own needs and abilities.

Frequently we fail to distinguish between different problems and needs. In adult education we face a problem like that we have in dealing with ourselves: We have to do the best we can with what we have. And many adult education situations are far from ideal.

The active life is the best. People will respond to appropriate action. We should try, where appropriate, to relate words and deeds; to help the learner understand that what he is learning may help him live a better life, help his fellow man, do a better job, or broaden and extend his horizons. Many adults will not continue to spend their time with words, words, words. Brother Lawrence, a seventeenth-century monastery cook, could pick up a straw to the glory of God. He learned and effectively practiced the relationship between what he did and what he knew.

The sooner we can adjust our system of education to people instead of trying to adjust people to our education system, the sooner we will strike a blow advancing the civilizing process. Adult education can tackle social and educational ills. Adult education can help change the system of learning, where such change is needed. It can help get people to understand education as a balanced, continuing process to help us discover ourselves, relate to others, recognize the relationships between subjects learned and the problems in life, and contribute our unique talents toward the creation of the social mosaic. Given the opportunity, many adult learners will respond to the idea that life is more than a frenzied scramble to earn money, to possess more, bigger, and better things. And further, adult education can help us understand the pettiness of the notion that when you've been to school, you've been educated.

The first step toward any such changes is to put the learner first—ahead of administrators, teachers, buildings, money, or computers.

Often the traditional, formal setting is not conducive to learning experiences that release the learner sufficiently to discover his own possibilities. Traditionally many teachers or professors have been status figures the learner approached with apprehension, if not fear. In such circumstances learning could not include experiences of creating, discovering, and releasing; but only a series of confining, pseudo-disciplinary exercises that often stifled and confused the learner. Charles Dickens presented this learning pattern dramatically in *David Copperfield* in the episode where David's step-father acted as his teacher. Standing before David with a switch in hand, the teacher would examine the frightened pupil. While physical punishment usually is no longer used to make sure lessons are learned, we often employ a weapon just as powerful and more destructive—chastening by psychological means.

Fear is indeed a potent teaching force, but it does not teach us what we need to know about becoming helpful, loving, maturing human beings. Formalized teaching procedures tend to isolate us from what we need most in order to grow—one another. Isolation and fragmentation are two of the greatest deterrents to human growth and development. One breeds suspicion and fear, and the other the inability to handle them. The result is that at forty, fifty, and sixty we are handling some of our problems much as we did when we were five and ten years old. The dangerous differences are that we have found ways to cover up our immaturities by misapplying some of the things we have learned in the interim.

Some of the confusion about living in today's world that is reflected in what we teach and learn is due to the fact that we have never been helped to know what we really should know. With the strong, almost overwhelming, emphasis on materialism taught and respected today, it is little wonder that some of the usual paradoxes and contradictions in life become so magnified that they are increasingly difficult to recognize and cope with.

We have a big job to do together. We can develop and participate in a system of continuing learning for adults dedicated to bringing our lives into some kind of balance and relationship with other people; a system that can translate and use the best the world's artists, scientists, philosophers, musicians and poets have given us; a system that helps us see each one of us as a precious link in the social chain rather than one of a mass of divided, confused units.

All this is based on the idea that we have to do something. We have to participate actively in the life of our social institutions. We have to assume a reasonable share of responsibility for the welfare and development of ourselves and others.

When we assume our rightful places as responsible citizens, we often confront many obstacles, many apparent or actual contradictions that may cause us to neglect our responsibilities or to make up our minds on insufficient evidence and thereby pursue a questionable path.

Generally speaking, we have difficulty in dealing successfully with contradictions and paradoxes. We prefer easy, clear-cut answers like yes or no. We feel better if things can be settled right now, so we can get on with the next problem;

but, when we stop to think, we realize many situations that occur in our lives cannot be settled as easily as we would like. Instead of taking time and effort to understand or solve the problems, we waste infinitely more time and energy bickering about them or nursing a sense of personal guilt and discomfort.

As I said before, we have tried to make education too easy. In trying to standardize and mechanize education we use the frontal, direct attack without considering the complexity of human development. For example, when a person is unable to cope with some family problem, this usually affects his job and all his other relationships. This is a well-known fact, yet not enough is done to deal with the whole person. Industries are unwilling or unable to use training that strikes at the whole problem, at how the employee's job efficiency relates to his whole life. We can be taught how to deal with people and how to improve our relationships through instruction on the job, as well or better than in a formal course called, "How to Deal with People."

The contradiction here is that we know what we do in one part of our life affects what we do in other parts, yet we compartmentalize ourselves and behave as if each institution is responsible for only one part of our life. The church sees to it that the immortal soul is nourished; the factory, that our vocational talents are employed; the home, that certain physical and social needs are provided for. Little effort toward integration is made by any of these institutions. The school follows the same pattern by offering a group of courses; the relationship of one course to another and of all of them to the learner is sometimes ignored.

This kind of contradiction causes the adult to waste time and energy. It makes him see life as composed of unrelated, isolated units. It fails to treat the adult as a special person seeking maturity through wholeness and instead encourages further fragmentation.

100

We must pursue a system of adult and child education that advances the kind of society we consider ideal and also helps us continually examine these ideals. Presently we are experimenting with a kind of social order that considers it necessary for each person to be an active, participating, responsible member with something to say about the social forces that shape the order. Clearly, we must strive to become an educated people or we'll have no society at all. We can't very well find many answers in an educational system that flourished three or four hundred years ago when relatively few people were responsible for the order of things. Some change in the system has obviously taken place; indeed, the change has lagged seriously behind the desire and demand for greater benefits from the social order.

Any system of education must fit the desired and existing social order, and ours fits only in part. When everybody has something to say about what happens and wants to say it, when everybody is to be free, then everybody must be taught how to use these privileges and learn to balance them with appropriate responsibilities. When more of us have an opportunity to take something out of our social order, we must be taught how to balance this by putting something into it. The success of a free society could well be measured by how well we are taught, and can accomplish, this delicate feat of balancing our giving and our taking.

It would be unwarranted to blame formal education or any other kind for all the problems of the adult or the ills of present-day society. To point to one person or situation or institution as being fully responsible for this problem oversimplifies the issue. Problems are the result of a complex constellation of factors. What and how we are taught does, however, loom large as a principal cause of the way we behave. Many institutions teach mainly by formal means of instruction, and a large share of responsibility for adult fragmentation must go to the way we teach children and adults in three of our major institutions: the home, the school, and the church.

A system of education must be suitable to the nature of the social order in which it exists. If we propose to develop the democratic idea, which characteristically holds that all people are involved in the determination of their social destiny, then a system of education where a very few people make decisions for the many would be inappropriate.

9. Originality and Conformity

A paradox that has caused many persons to modify their approach to life situations to the extent that their talents have never been utilized has been the admonition to strike out, be original, dare to do, but stay within the limits understood and approved by those who are often unoriginal.

High school and college commencement speakers for decades have hit hard on the "stand-up-and-be-counted" theme. They have told eager audiences that the world is in a mess and that the older generation is turning the torch over to the new generation. The implication seems to be that each generation has asked metaphorically for the next one to bail it out. But those of the new generation who take this counsel seriously sometimes discover that there is a place in society for the original thinker and nonconformist only so long as he fits into the established pattern of the institutions he joins.

In fact, many persons do not have the fortitude to withstand the constant resistance to change exhibited by some of their associates and institutions. The result is conformity and the consequent loss of many ideas that are not listened to at all or are politely heard and disposed of as eccentric. Often this restraint is defended by saying that worthwhile ideas will come out and this is a way to try them by fire. Sometimes this does happen. But this devil's advocate theme is usually nurtured in obstinacy and resistance to change.

102

More often than not it is an attempt to keep the old machinery running smoothly without interrupting it with a lot of adjustments. We spend much of our time trying to maintain our position rather than studying possible changes and adjustments in our situation.

Change comes slowly. Conformity swallows up many personalities and with them many ideas. All kinds of devices are used to stifle and discourage and put in his place the one who would do something different. No institution is free from this retarding influence on its own and the general social development.

Society and its institutions will evolve, will change. Yet this adjustment often proves administratively inconvenient. The unfortunate aspect, which can be corrected by effective learning, is that a citizen soon learns to "be a good Joe," to "keep his nose clean," in short, to conform, to follow the leader.

It is true that, if our kind of free society is to succeed, we must learn to obey as well as command. We must follow at times, but we must also offer leadership commensurate with our ability. We must be educated to make intelligent judgments, to bring leadership and followership into a working balance. For precisely this reason we need participation training in adult education to teach every adult the skills of leadership and followership.*

All is not lost in trying to cope with the problem of conformity. We can be trained to make better use of our talent. Many persons in authority accept and assess new ideas constructively; some industries actively encourage suggestions by offering financial and other rewards; but more must be done to encourage creativity and new ideas. Many of us neglect our responsibilities as citizens by failing to offer

* For a description of this kind of training, see *Participation Training for Adult Education,* by Bergevin and McKinley (St. Louis: Bethany Press, 1965).

new points of view, by not knowing when to conform and when not to, and by not being trained to know what our responsibilities are and how to discharge them.

When children are taught to conform in school and in college and on graduation day are told to "stand up and be counted," we are establishing a real problem for adult education. But it is a problem that can be handled. It should be attacked in the churches, in unions, in factories, in night schools and libraries, and in clubs and societies. When adults learn to "stand up and be counted," and to identify and discharge their responsibilities as citizens, they can teach this to the children and see that the schools do likewise.

10. ATTRACTING ADULTS TO LEARNING PROGRAMS

Two problems in adult education that require careful attention are, first, convincing the adult that he needs to learn continuously; and, second, developing ways to attract him to programs of learning.

Successfully to get and keep us in educational programs, the adult educator must understand our nature and be able to identify our needs and problems in terms of that nature. Then he must be able to translate what he discovers in this diagnosis into productive learning programs.

Most adult education programs are voluntary; and, when something is not obligatory, many of us find it difficult to arouse ourselves to do anything about it, even if our intentions are good. Self-discipline is one of the most difficult arts to practice. Freedom is necessary to the development of the creative spirit, but to distinguish between freedom and irresponsibility requires a kind of discretion some of us fail to exercise.

The voluntary nature of most adult educational programs presents a particular challenge to those who promote these programs. Adults have to be shown the value learning would

104

have for them. This can generally be accomplished in properly conducted adult education activities. Getting the adult to begin at all is the first big problem. Different programs, times, and situations demand divergent solutions.

Regardless of how socially idealistic we would like to think we are, we usually ask, "What will this do for me?" The successful adult educator will answer this question forthrightly. He will try to show the adult how he can be helped, how it will be to his advantage to become involved in the learning program. The perceptive adult educator knows he must start where the learners are—with their beliefs, emotional make-up, and educational backgrounds—not where he thinks they ought to be. Most of us are more concerned about ourselves than about others. But we can be taught to reach a healthy balance between our ego-centered and our socio-centered relationships. We have to be caught first, however.

A poignant appeal can be made by stressing the social values of attending adult educational programs. Many persons come to learning programs mainly to have some place to go and to be near other people. Women come to meet men, men to meet women; many come just to relieve the boredom they find in life. These reasons are as good as any to use as starters to get persons involved in learning.

The educator must make known to the potential adult learner that he is aware of some of his real needs and real problems and that the programs of learning will aim at satisfying these needs and attacking these problems. Generally adults are not concerned about problems they cannot understand or relate to personally. The adult educator shows the potential learner that he knows, or is willing to find out, what the learner's educational problems are, and that he cares enough about the learner to help him try to solve those problems.

Institutions can help attract the adult learner to programs

of adult education. As more institutions assume their share of responsibility for the education of adults and more people hear about it, more concern is exhibited among would-be learners. Most of us like to follow the crowd, to do what others are doing, or to do the "right" thing. Institutions can take advantage of this trait by offering well-planned and well-conducted learning programs and by advertising these activities widely.

Mass media (newspapers, radio, television, magazines) can promote the importance of continuing learning for adults through appropriate editorials, stories, documentaries, plays, and announcements. The mighty opinion-forming institutions represented in the mass media can, and to some extent do, promote and popularize the idea that a democracy cannot survive where people are uneducated and irresponsible, that learning can be interesting and valuable to the adult, and that the learning acquired in school as a youth cannot sustain a citizen of a democracy for the rest of his life.

The public schools can make a great contribution by assuming a large share of responsibility for the education of the adults in each community. This can be done not only by conducting their part of community adult education, but also by acting as a clearing house for other adult educational activities in the community. They can keep the public informed about many educational opportunities in the community through a continuous promotional program.

More ideas undoubtedly can be advanced to attract adults to learning programs, but every one of them must be realistic. They must exhibit a sound knowledge of the nature of the adult: his beliefs, hopes, fears, and aspirations.

11. LEARNING TO LIVE WITH TENTATIVE SITUATIONS

The nature of change and development makes solutions to some of our problems tentative. If we ignore or fail to recognize this situation, we create a barrier to adult learning. Seeking the security of absolutes occupies much of our time and energy. Most of us find it difficult to learn to operate with reasonable comfort in a provisional atmosphere.

We tend to go to extremes. Socially we either do very little for people or try to do everything for them. Political views range from anarchy to autocracy. Morals run the gamut from prudishness to licentiousness. In our own lives some of us want all the answers to every problem; others of us don't particularly want any answers. All of us have to learn that we need to find better answers to know how to live, and that our study will often reveal that these answers are known only in part. We have to be able to function with this knowledge while we seek a fuller solution.

We are seldom able to resolve a problem neatly and then proceed to the next problem and solve it too. This "state of suspension" that we must learn to live in confuses us. In some cases we become captious and bitter because we cannot have omniscience. In others we become indifferent and indolent; if we can't find a ready and complete answer, then why try for any?

Some problems for adult education are to stimulate the adult learner to find working answers to his problems to help him live comfortably with fluid and tentative situations, and further, to inspire him to seek to relate his search for personal answers to the larger search for corporate answers. Intimately associated with these problems is the attempt to develop in the learner an attitude that can sustain him through the struggle he will encounter in the learning adventure.

The productive use of any situation depends on our ability to select the most appropriate and useful of the extremes and bring them into balance. Problem situations to which every adult must address himself are rarely determined by a clear yes or no answer. We usually seek the easiest way

107

out of a dilemma and consequently are prone to follow the kind of leadership that promises positive results with absolute answers. This requires little struggle or thinking on our part. When this kind of leadership or philosophy fails us, as it often does, we seek other absolute answers or we suspect all answers and become cynical.

Adult education could help us greatly if we could be trained to understand that we often have to choose the lesser of two evils. On this premise we could develop a tentative but functional working relationship.

We have a perplexing problem before us when we try to bring things into balance, to seek an equilibrium. Much of the education we are exposed to contradicts this point of view. Often, this confusion is inadvertently promoted in our schools, by our mass media, and in our churches and clubs. In schools we sometimes learn that all you really need is a thorough grounding in some kind of educational program. Sometimes the programs differ widely, but each advocate tries to convince his following that the views he represents offer a saving balm to society.

Advertising, which seems to have made more practical use of psychological insights and behavioral patterns than many of our other institutions, bombards us with information. Too frequently professional advertisers misuse the knowledge they have about our nature. Clever interpreters of psychological and sociological information sometimes place ethics and their responsibility for social development in the background. These purveyors of information care little whether the results of their training campaigns promote maturity or immaturity in the learner as long as he absorbs television commercials or roadside messages. Evaluation of results is limited to determining how much the learner spends on the product promoted. This leaves much to be desired in our struggle to promote personal maturity and the civilizing process. Training people to buy more than

108

they need, to borrow more than they can afford so they can buy still more, to be constantly dissatisfied, to be the envy of their friends and neighbors is taking advantage of their social and psychological weaknesses.

Confusion of values results when other institutions, dedicated to helping human kind mature, advance a significantly different point of view. The noticeable result is that we separate our lives into incompatible compartments. We feel that the church handles certain problems, but much of the information we get from it is impractical in this day and age. So Sunday (for an hour or so) becomes the day some of us are religious. The rest of the time we have to be practical.

While most schools and colleges have become vocational training institutions, part of the curriculum is still designed to help us broaden our perspective. This part is often thought of as "stuff" that has to be taken in order to get through so we can get out and make a success of ourselves, success being measured in terms of possessions and the power we can exercise over other persons.

Certainly colleges, religious institutions, and social groups dedicated to advancing the civilizing process are making some progress. But colleges have a long way to go to make constructive use of known behavioral insights in interpreting the vast storehouse of knowledge at their disposal. Religious institutions also neglect to use much that is now known about the application and interpretation of their doctrines. Like the schools of higher learning they depend too much on enigmatic means to change people. The leaders of these institutions often have had little or no training in how we learn and how we can be taught, yet colleges and churches are two of the major educational organizations. Sometimes the personnel of these institutions show more interest in their subjects or doctrines than they do in the learners.

Motives differentiate institutions, and different institutions teach different things. Adult education is sorely needed to help us to bring some of these divergent philosophies into a workable relationship. We need help to try to develop a balance between making a living and learning to live. We need to know how to make our material resources serve us rather than use us.

These and other problems do not have immediate answers that we are able to understand and use. But some tentative answers are available from which we can get some support while continuing our search. Although the answers are tentative, one is not necessarily as good as another or so relative that anything is as good as anything else. In seeking to forward the civilizing process, some answers are much more effective than others.

Some facts and truths are not even tentative in nature. Some have not been discovered or revealed; some we do not understand; and some we know but choose to ignore. Productive adult education isn't an everything-or-nothing situation. We have to take what we can and make the best of it. Something is better than nothing. If this is to be our approach, we cannot race through subject matter at the rate of so many books, pages, or pamphlets each session, regardless of whether learning takes place. Since we are teaching adults rather than subjects, we adjust the program and readjust it as often as necessary to meet the special needs of the persons with whom we are working. This often means that the adult educator must be temporarily satisfied with tentative conclusions that, in the hands of intelligent leadership, can serve as points for refreshment, assessment, and careful planning for future attacks on the problems.

CHAPTER VI

Concepts to Implement the Education of Adults

The development of a learning program for adults must be founded on some belief, assumption, or philosophy that provides the support and direction for it and serves as a base from which one can evaluate the program as it progresses. The totalitarian operating in any area establishes an underlying scheme for his program that should make the learner follow orders and generally do and believe what others wish him to do and believe. Other persons are convinced that the principles of the totalitarian, wherever he lives or whatever institution he operates from, are incompatible with the development of human personality. Whether the lay or professional adult educator is totalitarian or abhors the despotism associated with this view, he must still have some kind of base from which he operates and that he can understand and make comprehensible to others. In this chapter a number of assumptions, guidelines, or concepts upon which a program of adult education might be constructed will be examined.

It is frustrating to the organizer of adult programs, as well as to those who participate in the learning adventure, to begin a program without careful planning firmly based on some established and understood principles and goals. Some of the goals are permanent; others change and are adjusted as the program progresses, depending on what kinds of problems arise in the dynamic learning enterprise. If positive results are desired, then a positive and fluid strategy based on sound objectives should be designed.

If used well, the concepts offered below could help us become more aware of our needs and responsibilities. These ideas can help us learn to grow, to discover our potential and use it. When intelligently interpreted and used by trained personnel, these guide lines can help us explore, understand, and pursue a democratic way of life.

The term "democratic way of life" means different things to different persons. To some it is the essence of goodness, the desired end they seek. To others it is a silly excursion into an impractical way of living, which will end in anarchical disaster. Some of us think of the democratic way of life and democracy as the same thing and we may mean a political system or a political party. Some of us haven't bothered to think about it much at all.

Democracy in the original sense meant the rule of the people. It was a political system in which every free or freed person could vote, and many did, on every issue that came before the ancient Grecian city-state of Athens. Actually, people gathered together in a stadium or amphitheatre and by a show of hands made their beliefs on particular issues known. It was not a representative form of political organization where people vote for a person who, when elected, represents a constituency and is supposed to determine its will and see that its will is exercised in the assembly of representatives. This representative system is a characteristic of a republic.

In a true democracy everyone has an opportunity to vote on every issue that needs attention, while in a republic the

112

elected representatives of the people deal with issues of government.

True political democracy is impractical, and the word "democracy" in a political sense has come to mean a kind of republic in which the supreme power is vested in the electorate and expressed by elected representatives.

Where political power rests is of the utmost importance, since this should largely determine whether humans are to be enslaved or released and helped to grow. In addition, however, to the political implications of the word "democracy," it has come to have a broader and more inclusive meaning in the term "the democratic way of life." This term means what "democracy" should do when it becomes the major factor in the social pattern. The democratic way of life offers those who participate in it opportunities to seek out and discover a way of living that meets their personal needs, with as few restraints as possible imposed.

The democratic way of life is an experiment in living together. Millions upon millions of persons throughout the world are struggling today to try to find the answers to civilized association through what is called the democratic way of life. We are trying to find out whether we can learn enough about ourselves to restrain our barbaric nature mainly with self-imposed discipline. We are trying to learn whether we can be free without violating the freedom of others; whether we can see ourselves as individuals yet with a specific responsibility to the corporate body, the whole of society. We are trying to learn how to recognize and claim our rights as citizens and how to exercise the responsibilities these rights require. We are trying to learn how to take our places, according to our abilities, in the several institutions that make up the fabric of this way of life, and to participate by bringing our talents to bear on our institutions. We want to learn to live as we like, so long as our likes let us offer others the same opportunities and freedoms we have; and we

113

should learn to order our lives so that we continue to discover and use our potential for growth and help others to do the same. We need to learn *together* to take proper advantage of our opportunities and make intelligent uses of freedom for the benefit of the growth of precious individuality. We are trying to learn to relegate force, either overt or covert, to a minimal role. We are trying to learn to offer each other the opportunity to live abundantly by discovering more and more about the nature of things and people, including ourselves, and thereby to mature into the kinds of persons it is possible for us to become.

These are some of the implications of the term "the democratic way of life" as interpreted in this book, and the concepts for adult education that follow are selected to advance this way of life.

These principles are theoretical in that they are to some extent speculative and in an experimental or developmental stage. They are also practical in that they can be applied and used at least in part. Their effectiveness depends largely upon whether we care to and are able to use the intelligence and the potential we have to make this way of life something to think about or something to enjoy.

There is no foolproof social order, anymore than there is a foolproof automobile. We have a vast amount of knowledge about ourselves, about the way we behave and the reasons for our behavior. We also have volumes of sound information on what we must do to live fully instead of merely to exist. But we have trouble trying to use the available knowledge.

Adult education is important when it helps us to translate, interpret, and put to use the best we know; adult education is of value when it can show us how to know and worship God through serving and understanding our fellow human beings; adult education is useful when it can help us get satisfaction from our work; adult education is vital

114

when it can help us learn self-respect and respect for others.

The driver of an automobile has to learn how to drive safely, and repeating safety rules will not of itself do this job. He finally has to learn to control himself and the automobile and apply the safety rules. Knowing about a way of life that could free us, and knowing about the need for adult education programs that can support that way of life is only the first step. We have to learn to use the vast storehouse of knowledge available to us.

Here are some ideas that should be considered when programs of adult education are to be designed and conducted to help adults see themselves as maturing beings seeking wholeness. These ideas are not treated in order of importance or in any operational order.

1. Adults Can Learn

Every adult regardless of age, mentality, race, sex, religion, size, or shape can and must continue to learn in order to fulfill his nature as a developing, maturing being.

A major problem in educating adults is persuading persons that it is to their advantage and to the advantage of their society that they continue to learn, and that they are able to learn new things that can help them cope with themselves and with the problem of life itself. That learning, schools, classes, and children are synonymous in the minds of many adults is readily evident when adult education is discussed. Many adults presently are involved in adult education programs other than random learning, but these persons are a small minority of the adults in the world.

If we were to look for reasons why adults are not involved in continuing learning programs, we would discover that both the adult himself and his society share responsibility.

Often the adult is not well enough organized to plan his time to participate in a learning program. Many persons will not take the trouble to discipline themselves to set aside a

115

period of time for private study or to learn with a group. Every conceivable excuse can be fabricated to avoid any actual exercise of the self-discipline necessary to carry out a regular program of learning. We are too tired, are not well, don't have enough time, can't find a place to study, see no sense in wasting our time with a study that seems to have no practical value, or don't like somebody in the group. Or: the teacher or leader is a smart aleck; somebody is trying to put something over on us; we're too old; we're not smart enough or too smart. The list could be extended greatly. To be sure some of the points may be partially true, but by and large the basic reasons are not those we mention. In truth we find it difficult to discipline ourselves. Discipline is something for others. We don't want to change.

Sometimes we don't understand the importance of continuing learning for adults so they may become responsible citizens—citizens who must constantly make decisions which require discretion and judgment, citizens in every station in life who must speak to problems in the family, in their vocation, and in their church and government. What we learned in school as children or in college as older youths merely set the stage for the solution of adult problems.

We can learn. We can learn to discipline ourselves as an initial step in the process of continuing adult education. We can learn to accept a share of thoughtful responsibility for running our homes, churches, and governments rather than complaining about the poor jobs others are doing while we are unwilling to learn to do a better job or to help those persons who have accepted responsibility and are trying to make a social contribution.

Another obstacle to adult learning is that the learner frequently thinks he is too old to learn. This is often not an excuse but an honest opinion. Older people tend to forget more easily and find that sometimes they must put forth a little more effort in certain kinds of learning experiences. Actu-

116

ally people can learn at any age and learn well. While students of learning have discovered some change in a person's ability to learn as he grows older, it is not enough to deter anybody who really wants to learn. As we grow older, our values change and our interests and concerns change. Too often these changes are interpreted by potential learners as problems of learning, when actually they should be revealed as problems of interests.

The individual and his social order must cooperate in this vital continuing learning adventure. Social organizations must provide attractive opportunities for adult learning on a broad scale. Every living adult should have an opportunity to participate in some kind of learning program regardless of who or what or where he is. Working adults, retired adults, sick adults in general and mental hospitals, incarcerated adults in prisons, smart adults and not-so-smart adults must use their potential as human beings. This learning is urgent because it is in our nature to have to seek some kind of satisfaction of our urge to grow, to move, to change. When we fail to discover even small parts of our ultimate constructive potential, we seek alternate sources for satisfaction that are not always in our best interests or society's.

Everyone is limited to some degree in the amount of learning he can acquire. We are limited in two major ways: by our capacity, our learning potential, and by psychological restrictions we place on ourselves. Our mental capacity or learning potential is what we have to work with; we can't do much about this. We must approach the problem of adult education realistically by admitting that some of us can learn better than others because some of us have a greater capacity for learning than others. We have little control over the restrictions this puts on our learning; but the psychological restrictions we place on ourselves are at least as important as those placed on us from other sources. We can learn to

117

make better use of what we have when we break through the barriers of indifference and excuses we have constructed around ourselves.

2. Adults and Children Have Different Educational Problems

Adults are not just grown-up children. While many of our actions seem to indicate a degree of maturity not greatly advanced over that of children, we are, nevertheless, different human beings than children. We have problems to solve unlike those of children; we are different physiologically; our personalities are further developed; and our experiences differ.

In the early days of adult education, one of the major prerequisites for teaching adults was experience in teaching children. School teachers were drafted into the service of the church to teach children and adults in Sunday School mainly because they were trained in teaching children. Paid positions in adult education in such institutions as industry, the church, and agricultural organizations were often filled by persons who were former public school teachers. Recently, the American government recruited many school teachers for positions dealing with the education of adults in foreign-aid programs. The general feeling was that, if you knew how to teach children, you could use the same ideas in teaching adults. The theory seemed to be teaching is teaching regardless of the pupil. This is probably an oversimplification of the situation, but it proved to be what actually happened. In the problem of adult literacy public school teachers were employed because, as one government executive put it, "These people can teach youngsters to read and write, why shouldn't they be able to teach adults?" And some were able to do both jobs, just as the general medical practitioner is able to do a respectable job in most illnesses of children and adults. But the tendency is toward some specialization, because the specialists are better equipped to interpret the knowledge available in most specialties. The reservoir of information about people is being increased at a rapid pace by such behavioral sciences as psychology, education, anthropology, and sociology.

A knowledge of the physiological and psychological differences between adults and children can help us find a realistic and flexible base for adult education and can result subsequently in a productive program of adult learning.

Let us examine some of the striking differences professional and lay adult educators should consider. At the outset we recognize that the job of living presents different tasks to the adult and to the child. Professor Havighurst has offered a useful idea in his concept of developmental tasks. These are called "basic tasks of living" that must be successfully accomplished if we are to attain a degree of completeness in our lives. An adult must face such tasks as these: creating a satisfying relationship between husband and wife, rearing children, making a living, making a home, and assuming certain other social responsibilities. Adult education must be directed toward solving these kinds of problems, just as children's education must be pointed toward helping children live successfully as children and preparing them for the greater responsibilities of adulthood.

A number of additional clues may help us identify an appropriate philosophy of adult education based on the nature of the adult as distinguished from that of a child.

Physiologically the adult may have more problems of hearing and seeing than the child. The adult differs in body size, which should make it obvious that he cannot always use the kind of educational furniture suited to children. But the obvious is sometimes overlooked, and adults are pressed into desks that may serve as psychological learning barriers by reminding the adult of school as a child as well as making it difficult to extricate himself physically. Chronic illnesses are the lot of many adults, and the difference of physical needs and biological drives is significant. Neglecting to consider these physiological factors will prevent one from taking the measure of the problem of adult education.

Another area to be examined is personality. The behavioral patterns an adult uses to adjust to his environment vary from one adult to another. Adults have different personalities, but there is also a significant difference between the personality of an adult and that of a child. While personalities are probably always in a state of development in our changing, evolving nature, yet the older adult is likely to possess a more fixed and rigid personality than a child. A child's behavioral patterns are going through more rapid change; as a consequence, a child will usually find adjustment to a different social environment easier than an adult will.

This tendency of the adult to try to hold to established patterns shows itself clearly in many programs of education for adults. They sometimes find new ideas and challenging experiences disturbing. These new experiences and ideas conflict with their wish to keep things as they are. Many adult learners would approve of an educational program that would teach more about what they already know and would fortify their present position so change would not take place or at least would not appear as such a threat to their make-up. There may be instances where a degree of this idea of adult education may be appropriate, but most adult education programs must fit into the nature of things, which is change. Programs designed to promote active participation that leads to inquiring into new ideas and ways of carrying on are necessary to thwart the lethargy and personality disintegration that go with aging. But the adult is able to learn and grow and change as long as he is alive. When these factors are emphasized appropriately, the adult

120

can continue to develop his personality and also contribute to his well-being and to his social order.

The adult and child learner also differ in their attitude toward time. When a child thinks of time at all, he sees himself as sort of an everlasting unit—something that will not end. Actually, he's not much concerned about time, except that it passes too slowly. He can't wait to be an F.B.I. agent or a space traveler. The adult wishes for more time or for it to slow up a bit. The adult sees or thinks he sees the end, the termination of his life; the normal child is wholly unconcerned about this.

Successful learning programs for adults will have considered this perspective: the adult wants something he can use in one way or another. Most adults have learned the necessity for patience. They have learned that to accomplish anything they have to stay with it. Their interest span usually exceeds that of children.

The adult learner often thinks he knows more than he does, and he feels threatened in learning situations. The adult looks differently on a teacher or leader than does a child. He does not view the teacher or leader with the awe and authority often associated with child-teacher relationships.

Experiences also differentiate the child and adult learner. Adults usually have had more experiences because they have lived longer than children; they have had different kinds of experiences; and they usually interpret their experiences differently than children. While many of these situations may not have contributed to the maturation of the adults, they nevertheless exist and must be considered with care and caution. Some experiences contribute to our well-being and the civilizing process, and others could destroy both.

Experience can be advantageous or harmful in life in general and to the adult learning process in particular. The

121

adult educator, like the learners, must eventually put adult experiences in proper perspective in the educational program. The learning team must be aware of the uses to which individual experiences can be put, and they must also be alert to situations where experience seems to slow up or harm the adult learner.

Out of some of these general areas differentiating adult from child (e.g., personalities, experiences, and emotional connections) come these ideas which may assist in giving appropriate direction and meaning to adult education programs:

1. Adults come to learning programs with a more definite "set" than children;

2. Adult personality is more permanently fixed for good or ill;

3. Adults have more emotional connections with words, situations, institutions, and people than do children;

4. Many adults bring negative feelings with them to the learning situation because they resent authority;

5. Adults are more under the burden of certain stereotypes like personality and belief than are children, who are in a more formative stage of development;

6. Inadequacy and failure is more likely to be in the forefront of an adult's mind than of a child's;

7. The adult may see new learning as more of a threat to the balance and integration he has attempted to achieve;

8. Most adults must rather quickly see more relevance and immediacy of application than children do;

9. A group of, say, fifteen adults will usually have more variations in skills, interests, experience, and education than a similar group of children. They might be considered more highly differentiated;

10. Adult attitudes are difficult to change. If learning is not shaped to fit, any change will be forgotten or rejected;

11. Learners always look at situations, not necessarily as they are, but as they perceive them to be.

An adult is motivated by reasons often quite different from those of a child. The adult's purpose for learning is different. Many adult learners place great emphasis on vocational skills and social status. While a few adults are concerned with just increasing their knowledge, these are not the average participants in adult education programs. Most adult learners are likely to be motivated by a more pragmatic reason.

3. Existing Institutions Are Effective Channels

Where is the best place to operate a program of learning for adults? The answer is: in every institution that makes up the fabric of our society. Factories, churches, libraries, unions, schools, hospitals, agricultural cooperatives are all responsible for the education of adults. Every existing institution will have to assume a fair share of responsibility for carrying on educational programs that will satisfy its special needs and, in addition, will help the adult see the relationship of the particular institution to other institutions in his social environment.

In Chapter Two the section called "A Structure for Adult Education" treats this problem in more detail.

4. Adult Education Programs Should Be Indigenous

An understanding of the true nature of the learner and of his basic spiritual, social, and physical needs in terms of his environment has universal significance for the adult educator. N. F. S. Grundtvig, the Danish poet, cleric, psalmist, and adult educator, seemed to have an unusual ability to cast away the nonessential and get to the root of problems that have inhibited the growth and development of the adult. He saw the Danish adult living in the nineteenth century largely as a product of his environment. The Danish peasant, he believed, was shaped by the soil he worked, the religion he subscribed to, the social order of which he was a part. He saw in the common man a great potential. Out of his profound insights came the folk-high-school idea, which has been used successfully by all the Scandinavian countries. He saw, first, that the education of adults had to have a reason to be; it had to be based on something more than immediate passions and concerns. Adult education had to be part of the very soil from which the people sprang. It had to reflect the language they spoke, the God they worshipped, the food they ate. An understanding of the moving stream of life of the people would determine the success of the adult learning adventure.

Bishop Grundtvig's idea was that man needed to be assisted through learning to identify and pursue three basic needs: the love of God, the love of man, and the love of the soil. The emphasis on these elements gave life and meaning to the education of adults in Denmark and left an indelible impression on adult education in many places in the world.

Although the ideas of Bishop Grundtvig were developed in Denmark and other Scandinavian countries, they are valid for application to other areas with some minor alterations. In our present day in Japan the "Three Loves" idea, inspired by Grundtvig's work, has produced some effective programs of adult education. Discovery of the needs of the adult learner and how those needs can be met in terms of the particular nature of the learner in his own environment has universal significance. The important point is that adult education must be firmly based on an idea of ecological substance if it is to make lasting progress anywhere. Merely knowing how adults learn, how to manipulate their thinking, or how to get them to support an idea they only partly understand will not long advance the cause of civilization.

Today in America it is just as vital to the success of adult education to know and take into consideration the ecological aspects of the learner as it was in Denmark during Bishop Grundtvig's time.

People will not necessarily respond to a learning program merely because it is good for them. To be truly productive, an adult learning program must be fashioned to solve the *peculiar problems* at hand in terms of the *particular adults* involved. People need training not only to teach adults but to develop a program that is indigenous. Adults engaged in studying a particular problem in one part of the country might have one kind of approach, while a quite different means would be found desirable for another group of adult learners studying the same problem in another location. When we are concerned about the indigenous nature of the learning program, some of the questions we need to answer are: What are the learners like? Why are they as they are? What learning procedures would be in keeping with their natures? What abilities do the learners have? Why is this program necessary for these particular people, at this place, at this time?

Adult educational programs must start where the learners are environmentally as well as intellectually. It would be folly to expect any group of adults to deal with complex mathematical or philosophical problems without first determining whether their background warrants such a program. The same would be true of the general make-up of the adult. Persons who are rural-oriented are likely to attack problems differently than urban residents. The area where we live puts its mark on our personality. The better the adult educator perceives this local situation, the more likely he is to develop a successful beginning for an adult educational program.

It would be well to recognize that the careful study and later development of an indigenous program could lead to something of a social disaster if the program were never extended beyond the particular intellectual environment that suited it at the start. Successful adult programs expand the learner's horizons. The program does, indeed, start where the learner is, but it moves him into larger views, different ideas, broader concepts. It helps the learner see himself, why he is as he is, and how he relates to others who have different views.

When a stone is dropped into a quiet pool of water, a series of concentric circles extend outward away from the small disturbance the stone created as it hit the water. This is analogous to effective adult learning programs. We start provincially with what we know and feel comfortable with; then we move outward. We need some place to stand while we get acquainted, but we cannot remain there long or the program will either wither away or become so tightly knit and exclusive that it fails to act as a liberating, a releasing force.

Another pitfall in developing beginning programs indigenous to the people and the area where they live, is the danger of believing that what now exists is right and is what ought to be. While this problem is related to the first one, it has a distinct characteristic of its own. The indigenous idea takes advantage of a strong motivating influence for adult learning. Adults will respond better to familiar ideas in familiar surroundings. But the learning would be a fraud if its sole purpose were to perpetuate what already exists. After long and careful study the perpetuation of some ideas and ways of doing things would probably be indicated. Tradition plays an important role in our social make-up. A productive program of adult education suited to the personal needs of the learner and the corporate needs of the group will reveal new ideas that can be used and new ways of doing things. What exists now is not necessarily the best. It should be subjected to careful scrutiny by the learners as they move to broaden their perspective. Yet changes or new things are not always good either. Progress can be a deceptive term. It is used at times to justify a point of view. Since it is a "good" word like "motherhood," nobody wants to be against it. But all change is not progress.

Indigenous adult programs do not stay where they begin. They seek a way to get started in harmony with the nature of the learner, and they move outward, helping us see ourselves and others through a variety of subjects or content. Actually, the indigenous principle speaks to both content and process. The content or subject matter of the learning program is determined by the need and nature of the learner; and the way a person learns, the process, will also be affected by the unique nature of the learner. This indigenous idea may apply both to how a person learns (process) and to what he learns (content).

5. Expectations Must Be Reconciled

What do the participants in an adult learning program think the program ought to do for them? What do they expect to get out of the learning experience? Everyone comes to a meeting or class or discussion for a reason. Some persons attend because they are required to by some authority; others come voluntarily. In each case the adult learner expects "to get something out of it." His expectations may be formed during the sessions, if he did not have any firm ideas about what to expect before he started. But whether the adult learner is correct in his expectations or incorrect, he usually has some ideas about the program and particularly about what it should do for him. If he attends on a voluntary basis, he probably comes with some positive views on the advantages he will gain from the experience. The learner's expectations may be far removed from reality or they

127

may be reasonably close. In any case the adult expects something, and his expectations must be taken into consideration.

The adult learner is not the only one who has expectations, however. Leaders and teachers have expectations, ideas about what should be learned and why. In addition to these persons the institutions represented by the teachers or leaders have anticipations, expectations of what should happen in the learning sessions. To add to the complexity of the situation, society itself has some over-all expectations, even if they are rather broad or vaguely understood. Actually, we have four groups to consider: the learners, the leaders or teachers, the institution, and society as a whole. These four groups cannot operate at cross-purposes if we are to conduct a successful learning program.

For example: In an industry that operates a variety of training programs, some of the supervisors in the offices and factory are asked to attend a supervisory training program on company time. The top administration has certain ideas of what the supervisors should do, and the administration wishes to communicate these ideas to the supervisors. The success of this program is going to depend on several elements, not the smallest of which is the way the company or top administration has been able to communicate its wishes to the leaders or teachers in the program, and through them to the learners. The company or administration knows what it wants to do or has certain expectations for the program. But the leaders and learners in the program also have expectations. To insure a degree of success *all* persons involved must be included in the planning process. Involving all parties in the planning process can help significantly to reconcile the various expectations sufficiently to bring about a good beginning.

A certain amount of grumbling sometimes accompanies adult learning programs, particularly nonvoluntary ones.

128

Discontent can be forestalled if the expectations of the learners are met even partially. Taking the learners' expectations into consideration at the program's inception will clarify and modify some of the vague hopes learners usually bring to a program. When the administrator learns to communicate properly with the leaders and the learners, the varied expectations of these three participants in the learning program can be brought into focus and sufficiently reconciled to get the program off to a good start.

In such a program society would also have broad expectations expressed partly as ethics. Society in general is concerned about how people are treated and how the particular industry can render a service to society. Technically, society as such may not be represented directly in this planning process to achieve reconciliation; but the planners would nevertheless need to know and do something about what is expected of them in a broad social sense.

An example of a voluntary situation might be a program in a church. Generally, the same problems of communication and variation in expectations exist in churches as in other institutions. The top administration expects the members to gain certain things in the adult teaching programs carried on. In a program on marriage the administrators wanted to emphasize how the parties in the marriage-contract relate to God. This emphasis moved from the head officers to the learners through some minor officials and teachers, all of whom had ideas about what should be done and how. The learners, however, wanted to discuss problems of relationships between men and women. Until the various functionaries and the learners could make congruous their several expectations, the program could not be truly productive.

Reconciliation of expectations does not mean that the learner tells others how to teach or necessarily what should be taught. However, it does recognize that the learner may have some useful ideas about the program that should be examined. Attempts to reconcile expectations will sometimes reveal that the learner's expectations are so far out of line with what is proposed, or with what it is possible to achieve, that radical adjustments need to be made. The time to uncover this information is before the program gets under way and before some learners become discontented and disaffect others.

The expectations of all concerned should be discovered and, if possible, reconciled, to obtain the harmony necessary to start the program off successfully.

6. Freedom Is Important in Learning

It is desirable to present the participants in an adult learning program with as many opportunities to select content, choose leaders, determine time, place, and length of meetings, and decide on procedures as is consistent with the well-being of the program. Freedom is a critical problem in adult educational situations. The proper exercise of freedom can make a learner feel that he counts for something, that he is important enough to make a contribution and be listened to. When the learner feels he is respected and taken in as a co-partner in learning, he is more likely to improve his power of perception and to learn better.

Freedom is basic in bringing about optimum learning. But the misuse and misunderstanding of freedom can destroy the situation it might have improved. Freedom is a potentially dangerous ingredient in a learning program as well as a needed and valuable element. It can be dangerous and destructive when it is limited to only a few persons; when, for example, the administrators and leaders are free to exercise authority, but other participants in the group are free only to accept the mandates of these leaders. Further, danger is present when group participants are free to do anything they want to do but do not have the necessary discretion and experience to guide themselves.

130

To be an effective force in the adult learning process freedom must be balanced with discipline and bulwarked with understanding. Unless a fine balance between freedom and discipline is reached, we may get a situation akin to dictatorship or anarchy. An example of the misunderstanding of freedom and its uses in group learning can be drawn from some group discussion meetings that have been conducted. Several years ago the group discussion educational technique was used by some persons to try to solve most of the problems of adult education. It was the answer. Although this technique has been used for many centuries in one form or another, it was treated as something new that seemed to be the only solution to the problem of choosing techniques in adult education. Many group discussion leaders and participants were untrained for the task they assumed. The main idea seemed to be to allow people to talk freely. By some process not clearly delineated problems would be solved according to the needs of the participants, if they just had an opportunity to express themselves about the problems. While this idea certainly has a kernel of truth in it, reaching the goal is not quite as simple as this sounds. With untrained leadership what often happened was that the most aggressive members of the group would gradually wrest control from the leaders, and the group would follow the newly established leadership. Freedom here was used temporarily to test the quality of leadership more than as a device to help every member of the group to understand himself, his fellow learners, and the content under consideration.

How much is too much is a perplexing problem in many social relationships. Throughout history the majority of the people have been free only to believe what the political and religious leaders have set before them. The people generally were not trusted by those in authority. Many kinds of people and institutions would conceal restrictions under the guise of freedom. Power is difficult for any person or insti-

131

tution to handle. Some of us who have power over other persons may mouth the words and ideas of freedom, but we find it difficult to make practical application of this concept.

In general those in authority are either better trained or more interested, or both, in the situation over which they exercise their authority. They feel a sense of responsibility the average person may not have. The average worker, churchgoer, or union member often does not have as much at stake as those in authority, so his interest is not as great. Seeing this, the authority figures sometimes resort to using subtle psychological means to get what they want accomplished. Psychology has been used as a cloak to conceal the manipulation of human beings. Rather than going to these lengths and playing a rather dangerous game with people, it would be more productive to release human creativity and talent by patiently helping people to learn to assume responsibility and to develop interests in keeping with the social weal.

Freedom, then, is not to be interpreted as license to do anything you want, any time you want to do it. Nor should it be limited to the few. Freedom is delicate. Its use must be taught to all. We can learn to make discreet choices, to distinguish freedom from anarchy; but we have to be free to carry on this kind of inquiry. In a well-conducted learning program for adults we can see the proper use of freedom acting as a tonic to enliven the participants and help them understand and respect one another, while at the same time it releases their best creative individual energies toward the pursuit of a common goal.

We are naturally inquisitive; we want to look into things. We can be taught to use this inclination to our advantage and to the advantage of society. But we must be free from unnecessary social and personal restraints. We must be free to succeed, and we must also be free to fail. Freedom does not give us just life's pleasures; we must learn to assume responsibility for the successes and the failures which may occur. But there are more advantages than disadvantages in the proper exercise of freedom. Before the educational advantages of freedom can be fully realized, we must learn what freedom is and how it must go hand-in-glove with responsibility and discipline.

CHAPTER VII

Concepts to Implement the Education of Adults (continued)

7. GOALS ARE VITAL

Each program of adult learning should have realistic, specific goals or objectives clearly stated in written form— a determinate statement of intent known and discussed by *all* participants in the adult learning program.

A premise of the philosophy of adult education propounded here is that the adult learner should have something to say about some of the forces that shape him. He should help set the goals of the learning program. This notion is predicated on the view that most of us are able to and should assume this kind of responsibility. Goal setting involving all participants is one way to teach us to share the work to be done. As we learn more about our responsibilities, we can better interpret our rights and privileges. We are better able to discern the delicate balance among rights and privileges and responsibilities.

The adult, then, should have something to say about the goals of his learning program and how to make use of subject experts and other essential resources. Learners must help to decide where they are going and how to achieve those goals.

When people become involved, they become concerned; and concerned persons are more apt learners. The blackboard or easel should be used at the beginning of the educational program so all participants can see how goals are evolved. This is a simple and vital step toward involvement. When everyone has something to say about setting them, the goals set are often more realistic than when goals are established by the administrators alone, realistic, that is, in satisfying the particular needs of the learners. The fact that some people did a thing a certain way is no reason to believe others can or should do the same thing in the same way. If we are helping one another be creative, discover ourselves, and release our particular talents for our benefit and that of society, then we should be offered opportunities in the teaching-learning transaction for the kind of participation and freedom necessary to accomplish this. Too often we are *told* to be creative in an atmosphere that does little to encourage creativity.

When goals are set, they must be attainable. They must state the desired outcome as accurately as possible at the time. Extravagant, farfetched goals that are impossible to achieve are sometimes suggested at the beginning of a learning program when some of the participants are overly enthusiastic. As the learning program goes on, enthusiasm may wear thin, and the goal set at the beginning may be difficult to accomplish. When the learners recognize this, their enthusiasm may diminish further. It is important to set a goal or objective that can be handled by the learning group in the time available and with the talents and other resources at their command. It is also well to recognize that goals may vary with different learning groups, even when the groups are attacking the same subject or problem.

How accurately the situation will be assessed depends

on the ability of the participants and the quality of trained leadership in the learning group. Participants can be taught to make a fairly reliable estimate of the relationship of their time and talent and available resources to the nature of the problem at hand and to set a reasonably realistic goal. Such skills improve with practice, and goals become increasingly realistic and attainable. Instead of trying to conquer the world's problems in one great leap forward, the more mature approach takes a small part that can be managed; then when that is accomplished, the goal is changed or adjusted to encompass the next realistic step.

Recognized achievement is a great encourager. When participants see they have accomplished what they originally set out to do, they are more likely to be motivated to continue.

While realistic goals should be set by the learning group, that is, all those who have to do with the learning program, it would be fanciful to believe that no direction or help is needed in this goal-setting process. Goal setting is a problem in itself, one that people have to be trained to do well. Participants have to be trained* to set reachable, realistic goals just as they have to be trained to assume their responsibilities in other aspects of this kind of adult education. It would be absurd to assume that people who have had no instruction or training in how to participate in a learning project could take over the program and succeed. But with a moderate amount of proper training, success can be achieved; and a kind of learning environment quite different from the traditional teacher-student relationship is realized. The learner can learn a subject and, at the same time, learn how to relate with others, how to help others, and how to begin to take his share of disciplined responsibility for what is going on. He can thereby make a significant contribution to his own maturation.

---

* See footnote on p. 55.

The advantages of realistic goal-setting by all participants are numerous:

a. Clear-cut, realistic goals that can be achieved give the learner a sense of accomplishment that is vital in motivating him to continue to pursue the program he is engaged in and in inspiring him to participate in other learning programs;

b. The participant is exploiting a variety of aspects of learning, not the least of which is to take his share of responsibility for what is to be done. As he helps to chart the course of the learning program, he is learning to assume responsibility by taking responsibility. He is learning to become an active citizen in the broadest sense by learning to work together with other persons;

c. Participants can learn to express their needs, to recognize the needs of their fellow learners, and to establish a goal that reconciles these possibly different needs;

d. In a give-and-take learning environment that accomplishes a working degree of reconciliation, the participants can learn to relate and work together in a common task;

e. A person who is concerned is easier to motivate. When he helps set the goal, he is involved;

f. The goal can be our road map. A realistic goal must be set if we are to know where we are going as a learning team. Accurate evaluation depends on a lucid goal. We need to know clearly what we are setting out to do so we can evaluate our accomplishments as the program progresses;

g. When a goal is set realistically and by all the members of the learning team, it is less troublesome to adjust it later, if necessary. The best laid plans need to be assessed and revised at times. Participants should be taught to establish a goal that can get the program on its way, yet be flexible enough to stand adjustment if change is required.

An unreachable goal set by teachers or leaders or administrators at the start of the learning program can easily des-

138

tine a program to failure. As soon as participants begin to believe that they can't manage what they were directed to do or that their needs as they understand them are not being met, they become disturbed and express this disturbance by being super-critical, dropping out of the learning program, seeking support by asking for a great deal of special attention, or passively participating without real interest or enthusiasm.

Participants are more likely to accept changes graciously when they have been involved in the original planning and they help make the changes. When goals are set by the administration, it is easy for learners who have been doubtful about the learning program to begin with to point out how they knew the thing wouldn't work. Accordingly, morale is lowered, and unnecessary obstacles are thrown up to inhibit the kind of learning originally planned.

Evaluation is simply a process directed to discovering the extent to which a learning team accomplished what it set out to do. Evaluation is predicated on a specific goal established at the start of the learning program. Without a specific point of reference in the form of a stated goal, evaluation would be impossible. Evaluating the adult education program, determining where it has failed or succeeded and why, is essential to its ultimate success. In addition to providing a means of measuring the degree of achievement, the process of evaluation can be a sensitive learning experience for participants in the learning program. Therefore, learners should be intimately involved in the process of evaluation as well as of goal setting.

8. Learning How to Learn Is Helpful

All adult participants should have some training in how to learn. The best that is known about adult learning and procedures of adult education should be developed into appropriate training programs and shared with all participants.

Regardless of the scope or nature of the educational program the adult learner should truly become a participant —a person who is dynamically involved in the learning experience, sharing responsibility for it with the other learners. Passive listening by the adult learner is not enough. He should help those who are operating the educational enterprise to survey the need, organize the program, conduct the program, and finally, evaluate the results of the educational work done.

While content is a vital part of each adult educational experience, it is not the total experience. A large part of the potential value of each adult learning experience is lost in traditional adult education class-type learning exercises. All learning activity for the adult should contribute to his intellectual, spiritual, physical, vocational, and/or cultural advancement. Each time an adult is exposed to learning experiences, one major criterion is whether or not the experience contributes somehow to advancing the learner's maturation by helping him recognize and pursue excellence. Helping a learner comprehend and accept a principle or concept, so some person or institution may make better use of him, violates the dignity of a human being. Adult education programs conducted for any purpose short of that described above are likely to discourage the learner or to confuse him or to enslave him intellectually rather than liberate him.

If we are to assist the learner toward the pursuit of excellence in every learning experience in which he is engaged, every known facility and resource that will make learning a creative, energizing experience must be employed. And the learner himself is a great resource.

Every learner, and this term includes all of the participants, needs training in how to carry on his special responsibility in the learning process. Proper training in how to in-

140

terpret and make sense of what is being learned, how to learn, and how to accept responsibility as an active member of a learning team makes a learning program complete when it is incorporated with appropriate subject matter. We should be helped to learn to discover and use our own potential. Forcing adults to learn because it's good for them or for somebody else denies the creative nature of the adult an opportunity for expression. Such violation is truly a tragic social and economic loss. Training us to take our part in the learning plan, to use our talents, and to participate productively, places us in a dynamic rather than a static learning role. Such training can facilitate the acceptance of our responsibilities as citizens.

An adult educator's first concern is with the learner. Content, material, resources for learning come next as these can be fitted into a learning program that satisfies a learner's need. A philosophy of adult education is incorporated here, a philosophy that puts the learner and his needs first and puts books, subjects, resources, buildings, planners, administrators, teachers, and the vast machinery of education in subordinate positions.

9. Needs Must Be Considered

An effective program of adult education should consider the needs and related interests of the adult learner and attempt to discover and meet his real needs as well as the needs of his social order.

Frequently the adult learner is exposed to a partisan view that attempts to teach him to do what somebody else wants him to do or thinks he needs. This view often disregards the needs of the learner himself, how he fits into the situation, and what the learning will do to help him become a more useful and complete person.

141

Several factors are evident when the learner's educational needs are not considered:

a. In its effort to accomplish a particular job the organization sponsoring the educational programs has lost sight of the individual as a person;

b. Persons responsible for the educational programs do not know what needs are or how to identify them;

c. Persons responsible for the educational programs fail to see a relationship between satisfying the learner's personal needs and the corporate requirements; consequently, equilibrium between these factors is not established;

d. Programs are measured in quantitative terms. The larger the number of persons in attendance, the more successful the program is considered;

e. The individual is considered less important than the group;

f. Learning programs for adults are established to meet the approval of a few influential persons.

We know we can do any job better when we feel we count for something, when we are thought of as persons who are really needed, when somebody has confidence in us and thinks we're good. Much organizational discontent can be traced to people being ignored or feeling that they are ignored or slighted.

Our present social order tends to equate busyness with goodness. The busy person whose life is completely wrapped up in his vocation is at once ranked as good. In some cases it is almost a breach of ethics to consider, outside the classroom, the whole life of a person—his vocational, spiritual, recreational, and cultural life.

With more and more emphasis being placed on vocational activities, efficiency, and computers, the individual human being is likely to be neglected. Supervisors become too busy with papers, reports, and cards to get to know the needs and feelings of the people they supervise. The misunderstandings that result are far out of proportion to their real significance. We do not function at anything like our potential when we are acutely or chronically disturbed, whatever the reason for the disturbance.

Since everyone likes to feel important, taking persons for granted and not giving them the recognition they need eventually becomes disastrous. When persons cannot get the recognition or satisfaction they feel they need, they seek other ways of "becoming somebody" or of satisfying their needs. People will struggle in a rational or irrational way to find recognition.

Often the actual causes of the irritations never get exposed because they are so trivial and seemingly insignificant that participants would be embarrassed to reveal them. We talk about more admissible problems in order to mask the real issues. And, of course, we fail to solve the real issues because we do not realize that we are treating symptoms as if they were real needs.

Certainly much employee-employer unrest occurs when the honor and personal feelings of one side or the other are injured. Economics is but one factor. How people feel about each other determines how both economic and all other grievances are dealt with. When the smiles and pleasantries evident at the conference table are recognized by both sides as a superficial camouflage of real feelings and needs, problems appear more complex and are frequently left unsolved.

Failure to identify or deal with a person's needs is not limited to employee-employer relationships. This example was used because it cuts across so much of American life. Indeed, ignorance of need plays a universal part in the failure to solve our problems and in the creation of others.

Indifference to the needs of others or failure to understand them is related to our lack of genuine interest in each other. Concern with our own preservation and pleasure

143

occupies a lot of our time; consequently, an attempt to deal with others' needs often gets a poor start because we are too subjective.

Identifying and solving adult educational problems can be most successfully accomplished by persons who are trained to assist people to see all the needs involved. To bring this about we should know what needs are and how to identify them. Further, we should know how to use this information by establishing a program of adult training that incorporates it. It would be helpful to distinguish the three kinds of educational needs: symptomatic, felt, and real.

(a) *A Symptomatic Educational Need.* A symptomatic educational need is a manifestation of a need a person considers real or genuine, although he is unaware that it is an indication of something else.

A symptomatic need may not be readily identifiable. An adult educational diagnostician looks for the educational problem; the symptom of the problem is also the symptom of the need. Problems and needs are different sides of the same coin.

A symptomatic need can easily mislead a person who is seeking a solution to an adult educational problem. For example, a director of religious education believed there were not enough lay leaders or teachers for his Sunday school. He solicited some likely candidates but could not secure enough persons to satisfy what he believed was the need. Persons who volunteered were rarely, if ever, trained in adult educational procedures. They were either school teachers or persons to whom standing before a group and speaking came easily. And a lot of speaking they usually did.

A great reservoir of leader-participants had never been tapped—the learners themselves. Most of them said they weren't "good talkers." If they but knew, this "deficiency" could be an outstanding asset in adult education.

144

What was needed was a participation-training program for all participants—leaders, students, resource persons—everybody. Out of this participation-training program an effective leader-participant emerged, and with the help of the other trained participants in the group, a productive learning program resulted.

As he looked into the problem, the director of religious education saw a need, a need he was unable to satisfy—securing more leaders for classes. But when he inaugurated a participation-training program for *all persons* involved in the educational experience, he didn't need leaders as such; he needed *trained learners*. When this was accomplished, the leadership he did need was different from the elocutionist-leader type, and a new leader-participant emerged from the group. When the real need was satisfied, the symptomatic need vanished.

In determining correct identification of a real need through its symptoms and, therefore, interpreting the symptoms correctly, the ultimate test is whether or not the symptoms disappear when the real need is satisfied.

(b) *A Felt Educational Need.* A felt need is one considered necessary by the person concerned. Such a need may or may not be actually necessary to the adult's educational development. It could be a symptom of a real need, or it could actually be a real need. Sometimes felt needs also express themselves as interests.

During the Second World War some persons who could neither read nor write were employed in factories assisting in the war effort. Manpower was scarce and employers took what they could get. With the cessation of hostilities employers could be more selective, and the illiterates knew they must learn to read and write in order to keep their jobs. This is an example of a felt need that is actually a real need.

Suppose a person believes that to become socially popular

will be a great advantage to him vocationally and may lead to a promotion. He takes dancing lessons and learns to play golf with the "right" people. Belatedly, he discovers that he needs to learn more about human relations and certain manufacturing methods in order to be promoted. This illustrates a felt need that is not a real need.

(c) *A Real Educational Need.* A real educational need should reveal something necessary that a learner actually lacks and can acquire through a learning experience.

Obviously, a learner would have to have a working knowledge of arithmetic if he planned to learn the carpenter's trade successfully. An example of a real but less conspicuous educational need is that an adult must learn somehow to relate himself to other persons if he is to enjoy a productive life. In both instances needs actually exist; they are real and must be satisfied if anything approximating success is to be realized.

Real needs are not immutable. Our environment, our standards of values help determine our interpretation of our real needs. In short, we acquire ideas and beliefs which become important directional influences in our lives. If we are to develop into successful social and individual beings, we must follow to some degree the standards set by the social order. Many of the real needs we can identify arise from the values we have been taught. If and when such values change, so will some of the real educational needs. These needs are real in terms of a certain social outlook, standard of values, or established policy.

The adult educator always has a difficult task to perform in satisfying adult educational needs. He must try to reconcile the individual's needs with those of his social order without stultifying the initiative and creativity of the individual. This is the critical problem we face in all corporate relationships. The individual must retain and use his singular char-

146

acteristics in order to make the kind of contribution he can make to the whole of society. Yet sometimes the uniqueness of a member of society gets out of bounds. Either society is not ready for the contribution, or the uniqueness may express itself in out-and-out antisocial acts. In these cases the individual is either dissuaded or restrained. Sometimes society's refusal to accept a new or different idea may be justified by the view that such an idea would act to destroy or injure the corporate body. For the sake of preserving the whole, the part must be restrained. At other times society or a corporate body temporarily refuses to accept one of its member's views because the new ideas do not fit into an established or traditional pattern that is held to be true or workable. This case may be temporary because most "truths," if true, will eventually be understood by enough members of the social order to incorporate a change.

If the adult educator is concerned to promote the human maturation process, one of his prime tasks is to consider thoughtfully this difficult issue: how to arrange programs of learning so they offer the individual opportunity to experience the satisfaction that comes with freedom to explore new ways and new ideas, and yet provide the learner with an adequate working background in the old, the traditional, so he can discern their value.

Many of our needs and interests are related to our values. Tradition plays a vital role in establishing values; some are in keeping with the nature of things and some tend to impede development. The fact that something has lasted a long time is no absolute indication it is good. Nor can we say that something new will solve our problems merely because it is new. Adult education can promote the weighing of evidence, the studying of new ideas, the practicing of making more discreet value judgments. A prime objective would be to learn whether or not we are in tune with the nature of things in a broad and developmental sense.

How much is too much has always been a perplexing problem. It cannot always be solved exactly, but some of us are, or can become, more skilled at solving it. We can be taught to identify our needs, to reconcile our needs with those of the social order, and to improve our ability to make discreet judgments.

The adult educator needs to identify and understand some of our basic needs and consider them in each adult educational endeavor. Such a fundamental need as a sense of fulfillment or the satisfaction of succeeding in some enterprise or other is essential. Further, our needs to love and be loved and to establish and maintain satisfactory social relations with others should be recognized as vital to our continued growth. Needs of this nature must be considered in any kind of adult educational program that purports to succeed. The adult learner is not a different person when he is improving his vocational skills than when he is in church. He may behave differently outwardly, but he is essentially the same being with the same needs.

10. Problem-centered Learning Is Basic

Adults become more interested in learning and are more likely to learn when they are dealing with problems and situations with which they are concerned and in which they can identify related needs. The problem-centered or situation-centered adult learning approach differs markedly from the subject-centered approach. In the first instance the adult learner sees, or believes he sees, a need for learning something. It could be to learn to read better so he can get a better job, to grow beautiful flowers so he can receive the plaudits of his friends and have the fun of doing something creative. The potential adult learner finds himself faced with a real or imagined problem or situation about which he needs help in the form of instruction. Programs of adult learning

148

should be developed around such situations or problems as much as possible.

The alternative to this is the subject-centered approach. This often wasteful procedure seems to assume that particular subjects *per se* are good for adult learners, and somehow an adult can extract from these subjects what he thinks he needs to know. We are often unable to select what is useful to us out of the total information offered in a course, and help is seldom extended to the individual student to bring this about. We respond best to personal treatment, and some educators and most courses and subjects can be very impersonal.

Programs of learning for adults must be adjusted to the learners, to the problems they need solved, to the situations confronting them. Adult education must start there. As the learners' horizons are extended, the learning programs can be adjusted to them. The average adult learner functions in the realm of reality more than in that of abstraction, and a problem-centered or situation-centered program is real to him.

11. Resources Should Be Appropriate

The term "resources" is used here to mean materials, such as books, charts, graphs, films, maps, newspapers, and magazines, from which the adult learner can obtain information to supplement his learning experiences. Resources also include physical facilities like buildings, rooms, and desks. In addition to these kinds of resources, there are resource persons who are versed in certain areas of knowledge and who may provide helpful information. These persons may be called upon at appropriate times to share their knowledge with the other participants in the learning group.

Resource persons and resource materials are usually available for all kinds of adult learning programs. The proper selection and use of resources can be an interesting and rewarding activity for alert adult educators and participants who are willing to expend some effort. Since most adults attend educational programs on a voluntary basis, it doesn't take much dissatisfaction for an adult learner to quit. The adroit use of resources can keep interest at a productive level.

When text material is unattractive and the type is small, the average adult learner may become discouraged. Apparently, many books are not printed for the adult reader. Type is often too small or unclear for the older reader. Sometimes the color or finish of the paper fatigues the reader. Since it is not easy to get and to keep adults in learning programs, care should be taken to select materials appropriate to the physiological and psychological problems peculiar to adults.

Nearly everyone has had some experience as a learner in school. We have all been to school, and we tend to associate all learning with our childhood learning experiences. When we think of going to school, we think of children, desks, teachers, and the machinery of education for children and youth. Most thoughtful people admit that adults cannot carry on forever with the education they got as children and youths. Nevertheless, the school is still synonymous with the child. This view is deeply set in the minds of most adults. Adults will laugh uncomfortably when they talk of themselves as students or persons "going to school." Most schools and colleges of education have given relatively little attention to the problems of educating the 125,000,000 American adults. This picture is gradually beginning to change, but it changes very slowly.

Adults are sometimes asked to occupy seats so small they can scarcely get out of them after having managed to squeeze in. Even institutions other than schools may pattern adult meeting rooms after the childhood classrooms the administrators of the program remember. In many cases this picture is changing and physical resources more appropriate to teaching *adults* are being used. Desks and tablet-arm chairs set in rows are giving way to tables arranged so people can see one another face to face. Since many adults do not see or hear as well as they used to, resources must be selected to try to compensate for these deficiencies.

Resource persons also should be selected to supply expertise appropriate to the group and the subject. These resource persons should be instructed in advance regarding the nature of the group they are to be with and the task they are to perform. They should be kept from making long-winded speeches and, if possible, from showing off.

Adult learners are often sensitive about their role as learners. They don't want to be treated like children or use resources that smack of childhood learning. It is true that we sometimes do not know much more about things than do children, and we sometimes act at the same level of maturity as children; yet our image of ourselves is that we are grown-up and superior to children. Unless we recognize this situation, we can easily alienate the adult learner and negate our opportunity to help him learn more about himself as a step in the maturation process.

An important question about resources must be asked to insure the proper development of the adult learning program. Do the resource persons and all of the resources to be used fit the needs of the *adult* learner and the particular subject being considered?

12. A PROGRAMMING CYCLE SHOULD BE A COOPERATIVE EXPERIENCE

The programming cycle involves planning, organizing, conducting, and evaluating the adult educational program. Each participant in the learning group should help, so far as he is able, in each of these steps. This work is as important as the content itself, if the educational program is to take

151

full advantage of all of the learning possibilities that present themselves. Participation in the several phases of program development is in itself a valuable part of the learning experience.

Giving the participants a share in the programming cycle is often neglected or thought unnecessary. This is partly because many adult educational programs are controlled by a small group of persons who have planned the program, set the goals, and want to do any evaluating themselves. This means of operation presumes that the administrators or central planners know what is good for the adult learners and can, of course, determine whether or not the learners got what they were supposed to get at different stages of the program. But when the learners are left out of any aspect of a program, the administrators are not making use of all the possibilities inherent in the program. Many important things can be learned in addition to the subject under consideration. A dynamic program uses a subject as content and also as a vehicle to help participants learn to know each other, to determine needs, to set goals, to make an evaluation, and to assume a degree of responsibility for this whole process.

There are several important reasons why the learners should be actively involved in the programming proceedings. Three reasons follow:

a. Learners need to become part of a situation if they are to develop and maintain an active concern for it;

b. Planning, organizing, conducting, and evaluating are organized procedures, take time and effort, and can give the participants opportunities to learn something of discipline and responsibility by inspiration rather than by imposition;

c. Many untapped resources available among the members of the learning group can be utilized.

Nothing is quite as boring to most adult learners as having to sit hour after hour and listen to somebody tell them what they need to know or what he thinks they need to know. This passive learning situation does not bring out the best in most adult learners. Programs of adult education have been ruined because persons who conducted them used the same methods in dealing with adults that they used with children.

The adult is often a volunteer; he can quit a class or learning program when he wants to, and he often does. Many adults will not come to programs of learning at all; they say they aren't interested or don't have the time. A host of other reasons are also given, many of them merely symptomatic. Actually many adults feel that they aren't in the programs; that something is being poured over them just as it was when they were kids; that they are being indoctrinated, not educated. Now that they are adults they should have something to say about what they do.

Sometimes this view is valid and sometimes not, but it is, nevertheless, a factor in the success of adult educational programs. The adult learner almost always has something to offer if he is actively involved and if the adult educator knows how to help him reveal and use his talents. While participation in the programming cycle is only one means of involvement, it is an important one. The adult learner can be helped to feel he has some stake in the project.

Participants will become actively concerned and involved when they are *helped* to share the management of the program with fellow learners and readjust the program to point to the goal and to participants' recognizable needs. We don't learn to be free, creative, disciplined persons only by being told this is what we ought to be. We learn this by being exposed to situations where we have to make choices based on information we have acquired or are acquiring. Too often we are not given any opportunity to assume responsibilities

153

and, therefore, we can't very well learn to assume them. If people can't be trusted, then the idea of democracy is a delusion.

As children, most adults were told what was "right" and "wrong," what to do, and when to do it. It is easier for most of us to continue to follow the directions of others and therefore avoid any problems that might occur if we were to try to think for ourselves. But adulthood is not childhood. We have different experiences and different needs. The independent thinking we need to do in order to contribute our particular talent is often not done because we've never been taught to do it. We continue to let others think for us. A good deal of the "original" thinking we are taught to do is only to learn subject matter and try to relate it to our problems so we come out with approved conclusions.

While society must depend on proper authority properly exercised, most persons are not concerned with the nuances surrounding the use of power and authority. They have found it is better for them if they are left alone; so long as they aren't disturbed too much, they'll do the boss's bidding vocationally, politically, and spiritually. Many of us have been trained to follow and sometimes do so unconsciously even if it means neglecting our responsibility to think and study and evaluate issues as members of a society struggling to understand the meaning and use of freedom.

If a society did not depend on the average person's ability and willingness to take his share of responsibility for its development, it would be unnecessary for us to be concerned about disciplined, responsible citizenship or the broad and continuous education of adults. But our society is based on having each citizen take a reasonable share of responsibility for how things are carried on. Either through indifference or past training or both, we tend to be content to let others take over responsibilities that should be

154

ours. Most of us adults need to learn to discipline ourselves and to use our latent resources for our benefit and for the benefit of our fellow citizens. Some of this can be accomplished through adult education. It can be seen that adult education is both a patching process and a means of enlarging horizons and presenting new and challenging information. In some cases, it is patching the education the adult received as a child at home, in church, and at school— education that often had little to do with helping the child learn to assume his later responsibilities as an adult living in a free society.

Since the child had little to say about what went on in school, the adult is supposed to have little to say about his continuing education. Now and again, he is asked to act grown-up, but he doesn't know exactly what that means unless it means to dominate others, be aggressive, drink, or smoke. Many of us are little more than big children—persons who have larger bodies than children and who are trying to reconcile our childhood training and experiences (some of which may have suited our needs at the time) with our present needs. The outcome is often bumbling and tragic.

We can do something about this problem. We can begin to learn to grow up. Some of us who are willing to try will first look for a course in growing up or for something like one with a more pretentious name. Even if such a course existed (and some institution would undoubtedly put such a course in, if twenty persons could be gathered together to take it) it would do little to help a person mature. We learn best by taking part, by sharing, by feeling we are part of the situation in any learning experience. We can be helped and inspired, rather than forced, to do our share by being given intelligent direction and an opportunity to express our opinions and make decisions. Sharing responsibility for adult

155

learning programs we are involved in is one productive way to give us some experiences we need in order to learn to grow and develop.

Adults generally have more talents and capabilities than they use. Resources are available, but it is often difficult to bring these resources into use. Frequently we are not sufficiently inspired by or concerned about a particular task to use what is available. We haven't been taught to discipline ourselves or we haven't tried to discipline ourselves or both. Like many personal problems the problem of discovering and utilizing resources is not all personal. While we need to help ourselves discover our potential, we also need the help of our fellow learners. Given the opportunity and instructional help in a group learning experience, the average participant can contribute a surprising amount to an enterprise like evaluation. If those in charge of the program are patient and persistent, the participant can be drawn out to say what he honestly thinks about what he has been doing and why he thinks as he does. Often the remarks made by the participants need to be evaluated to separate wheat from chaff. But as the learning program progresses and more planning and evaluation periods take place, a real change will be noticed in the quality of the remarks made by the participants. This change will take place because, as the opportunity for effective participation increases, so generally does its quality. People gain more confidence in themselves when they are listened to with respect and understanding, even if they are wrong or fail to use the best grammar or the most delicate phrasing. They are gradually learning how to do something by doing it. They are learning that others will help them and that they, too, may help others accomplish a common goal.

Unfortunately in many learning situations the participants are never given an opportunity to express their feelings about the work being done or the program generally. The participant gets no chance to discover himself. We need to know how to use what we know as well as how to learn more. Using the variety of talents existing in every group helps us to learn about each other, and having each person contribute something helps the group. Even if that something seems small, it is very important and should be treated with respect. If we can help each other use our talents to be responsible for the learning program we are engaged in, we will be more likely to make a success of the venture.

CHAPTER VIII

Summary and Conclusion

The philosophy in this book advances the notion that we are developing, evolving persons in a state of being and becoming and that it is in our nature either to destroy one another or to contribute to the civilizing process by making a continuing effort to become more mature and to seek fulfillment as social beings with unique personal characteristics that are to be preserved and related to the common good. The direction we move in will depend on what we are taught about ourselves, about other persons, and about our reasons for living—our goals and purposes. How we go about this job of living will depend on our values and our interpretation of those values. Learning plays a pre-eminent role in our development or disintegration as human beings. In one form or another the continuing education of adults can determine our success in mastering the problems of personal maturation and social relationships.

The following pages present some brief statements about the major propositions of the philosophy of adult education treated in the preceding chapters. The statements are ordered under six major headings. These summarize and bring together in condensed form those ideas around which an effective program of adult education might operate.

1. THE NATURE OF OUR SOCIETY

The society we live in is often referred to as a free or democratic society. A variety of meanings attach to the words "free" and "democratic," but generally we understand these terms to mean that the people who make up the society have something to say about the way it functions and that these same people are free of unnecessary restraint and control. Thinking beings need to be free to struggle with and try to solve the multitude of problems the developing adult encounters. Freedom to carry out activity of this sort sustains the adult maturation process. Individual freedom, restricted only when it comes into conflict with the welfare of the social order of which the individual is a part, seems to be essential to creative activity and the development of each person, since freedom can present each person with the opportunity to contribute his particular share to the common good.

But the problems of freedom and of a free society are many and, paradoxically, are created by those of us who need freedom. Here as in many cases, we are our own enemies. We are ego-centered and often over-concerned with our own welfare, even at the expense of others. Because we harbor a variety of fears, we seek security and often our quest for security separates us from others when we abuse the privileges and freedoms we have. We all need to feel we have some purpose in life; we seek some kind of fulfillment. Many times we pursue this need of fulfillment by putting undue faith in materialism and by surrounding ourselves with "things." The more we get, the better we feel—temporarily. We are also ambivalent creatures. This appears in our desire to be individualistic, yet to be part of our society. These seemingly irreconcilable desires have to be reconciled.

160

The problems of a free society are manifold, yet we grow and mature and contribute to the development of the civilizing process as we learn to work together to resolve these problems.

We who constitute our society are adaptable, educable persons who change and can grow as long as we live. While our society forms us, we also help to form our society.

2. THE NEED FOR ADULT EDUCATION

Since we have the great opportunities and the awesome responsibilities a free society offers, it should be clear that continuous learning is necessary if people are to live in community, manage their own affairs, and have something to say about the operation of the society of which they are a part.

Just living does not supply the information we need to be politically, vocationally, spiritually, and culturally competent. We know only a part of the answers to our personal and social dilemmas. But we have learned that by becoming involved, by participating, by contributing our share to the whole of society, we grow as individuals and help the social order. We know, further, that this is not a job for the select few. It is a task that must be assumed by every member of a free society, if that society is to continue to be free. Freedom in this sense is a highly relative term—related directly to the amount of constructive and responsible effort that every citizen is willing to apply toward its preservation and advancement. We learn to accomplish this by helping to establish and to participate in organized programs of learning, or through personal reading and study that broadens our perspective. We complete the process by putting our newly acquired information to use, intelligently and discreetly.

A broad, continuous, and appropriate program of adult

161

education for everybody is a necessary component of democracy.

The fact that most of us have spent years in school has at times acted as a deterrent to the extension of purposeful learning in the adult years. A series of educational experiences in our early life is thought by many of us to be enough to sustain us intellectually for the rest of our lives. Some of us really believe we need to know more but are actually ashamed of going back to school or attending adult learning programs of any kind. Inappropriate humor is directed at times toward the adult who participates in learning activities. Some adults have wrapped their books in newspapers so no one would know they were attending learning programs. Fortunately, many persons either do not feel this way or get over this embarrassment. In any case, those persons concerned about the civilizing process must exert a continuous effort to impress upon the adult that his world is changing, that he has specific responsibilities as a citizen of an evolving society, and that the schooling he received during his younger years is not sufficient to maintain his position as a citizen of a democratic society.

3. Definition and Nature of Adult Education

If we see our society as an evolving, developmental order attempting to offer the individuals who compose it the freedom necessary to grow and express themselves as creative beings, then it follows that we have to have the knowledge needed to function in such a society. We must learn to play our important roles as free and responsible citizens. Since we are involved in this continuing, evolving process, our learning needs as adults are continuous and changing. What, then, is this thing called adult education that we all need?

Education for adults can be any kind of learning that adds to their fund of knowledge, changes their attitudes or views or opinions, broadens their perspectives, or alters

162

their behavior. It can be the organized-classroom or school type; it can be an independent program in which the learner directs his own study; or it can be a group effort called participation training. These three types may all be classified under the heading of Systematically Organized Programs, as in Chapter Three.

In addition to systematically organized learning there is another kind of adult education, referred to in this book as Random Experiential Learning. This term includes the unorganized learning experiences to which each of us is continually exposed. Television, newspapers, conversations, reading, entertainment—everything we do has some effect on us, whether we are aware of it or not, and therefore can be considered a kind of adult education.

The program of study that trains professional educators in the discipline of adult education is concerned with learning how to teach adults, how adults learn, and how to assemble the machinery of the adult teaching-learning process to develop suitable and productive adult education programs.

The education of adults can be "good" or it can be "bad." It can be an activity that teaches us to weigh, to evaluate, to improve our ability to think and act intelligently about the events confronting our social order and us as individuals. It can help us try to consider and care for others in our pursuit of excellence. It can teach us to assume our share of responsibility in our jobs, in our homes, and in the several social institutions that constitute parts of our lives. Conversely, adult education can teach us to hate, to destroy, and to ignore the views of others. It can teach us how to manipulate other people to our advantage by using some of the very psychological insights that might be used to release us. It can teach us to be haughty and arrogant.

The *kind* of education we promote determines whether we grow and mature and become creative, loving persons or whether we inhibit creativity and misuse our potential by attempting to make robots of one another because we fear that differences mean badness.

When we are admonished to support or participate in programs of adult education, we need to know what kind of education is being offered. Is it designed to help us expand our horizons, to help us mature? Will it encourage our need to discover and to create or will it stifle or intellectually enslave us?

4. Goals in Adult Education

Learning programs for adults should begin with careful discussion and establishment of the objectives or goals of the venture. The persons who administer the program and all the other participants must be involved in this procedure, and each participant should have some understanding of what the program is supposed to do and what level of achievement is desired.

There are two kinds of goals: the overall, general goals of the education of the adult and the goals of the particular program. The overall goals are of a universal nature, while the individual program goals are more limited. The goals of adult education discussed in Chapter Two have to do with bringing the adult into an understanding relationship with his fellow human beings, with his environment, and with his own potential and purpose. The goals of a specific program should clearly indicate the end toward which the particular learning experience is directed. All goals should reveal an intention to meet a discovered need.

When programs are being organized and constructed, the general goals must be considered and incorporated in the particular program goals. For example, when industries or labor unions or churches plan their educational programs, they will have clear-cut intentions, plainly stated, for each program offered; but they must also consider the way these

164

programs relate to the overall goals that advance the citizen and his social order. To ignore these and to pursue only limited objectives would be to default in their social trusteeships.

5. A Structure for Adult Education

Adult education needs a pattern of organization through which it can function. The dangers of provincialism and a narrow outlook can be reduced if adult education is not controlled by any one institution. All institutions can and should develop programs of education for the benefit of their members. This would involve all the institutions that make up the fabric of our economic life—those on the farms, in the factories, and in the stores and offices of the nation. It would also include those institutions whose major emphasis is on the spiritual life of the community. Programs of adult education should also be carried on by mental and general hospitals for their patients, for their workers, and for the general public. The hospital should become the health-education center for the area it serves. Schools, colleges, libraries, clubs, and societies of every kind should assume their share of the important task of education by offering programs to which each is particularly suited.

Such a broad and general dissemination of adult education can assure us that no one group will dominate or restrict the free flow of information and ideas so necessary to human growth. It is also noted that frequently people have a degree of loyalty toward an institution that makes it easier to get groups of potential learners together. In every locality adults have access to at least one, and usually several, institutions that should be offering educational programs. Finally, it is the responsibility of every institution in a free society to do its part in this vast enterprise of continuing education.

6. Adult Education Programming

In order to achieve the goals indicated in Chapter Two any programs developed should take into consideration the following points:

Most adult education programs should be voluntary. The more we can persuade people to attend on their own volition, the more likely they will be to bring with them the right feeling about the program; this in itself encourages learning. It is sometimes difficult to discover and facilitate ways of attracting adults to educational programs. In the long run, the voluntary approach will prove more beneficial to the learner and to the sponsor than the use of force and threats, even if these are cleverly disguised.

The needs of the learner must be discovered, considered, and met. Programs must be designed for those involved in them. We must try to answer the questions the participants are asking, and we should help each other know what kinds of questions to ask. Successful adult education programs should not be designed for the convenience of the administrators or the institution but rather for the benefit and enlightenment of the learner.

The resources used for every program should be appropriate. Many kinds of resources for adults are available in every interest area. Books, newspapers, magazines, films, trips, and knowledgeable persons are examples of available assistance. A variety of appropriate resources suited to the particular situation at hand makes the program more interesting and can be an effective aid to learning. Careful attention must be given to the standardized type of materials issued by the central offices of many institutions. Sometimes these materials can be used to fit certain aspects of the learning program. Sometimes they do more harm than good by making the local leaders feel their jobs are easier than they actually are. Often this published material does not fit a local need at the time the need arises. There is no substitute for *trained* personnel at the local level who can help diagnose the local problems and apply the proper resources when they are needed.

Problem-centered or situation-centered learning is meaningful to adults. Inert ideas and subject matter only partially related or sometimes wholly unrelated to the problems of the adult learner discourage him. He must see some reason or purpose for what he is doing, and he can see this in terms of his ability and needs. If subject matter and other resources are woven around the problems and situations the learner has experienced, then they can relate to any new ideas presented to him. To offer a subject and expect the learner to do all of his own integrating and to see the relationship between the subject and his problems is expecting more than the average adult learner can handle. "Taking a course" and expecting that some day the learner may see some relationship between the subject and a life situation, has little merit as a means of changing attitudes or behavior.

When we are taught through problems we have, situations we have experienced, or needs we have identified, we are engaged in active, meaningful encounter. In this way of learning, we are not merely memorizing some "good" material hoping to be able to recall it, if the occasion arises. Rather, we start by helping each other fit the information needed to the level of our experience and comprehension, and then we move on into new, unexplored areas of learning.

We are concerned about tens of millions of adult learners, not just the relatively few who are interested in learning because they like to learn. The great majority of adults must see some reason for learning. Whether adult education is vocational or related to religion or the arts or studies about the

167

world we live in, it can hold the adult if he can see it in terms of situations he can comprehend, needs he has, or problems he wants to solve.

The programming of adult educational activities should be a cooperative endeavor. The adult learner will respond with more enthusiasm if he is treated as a full partner in the educational enterprise. The learners have had a variety of experiences that can be shared to advantage. It is unlikely that every participant will take an active part in the planning, organizing, conducting, and evaluating of the program. Timidity and inexperience inhibit full cooperation. But the more the learners are encouraged to help in the total operation, the easier it is to get an increasing number involved. Learners should be helped to see that they are needed and can each render a particular service by learning to work together in every facet of the educational program. Also, when the learner is involved in the whole programming cycle, it is easier to discover and meet his needs; and he, therefore, is less likely to be destructively critical of the activity.

When participants assist in the several phases of the programming cycle, they can realize more benefits from the time they spend. They are involved not only in learning a particular subject, but also in two other important tasks: learning how to accept and discharge responsibility and how to work with others.

Most persons concerned with an educational program have certain expectations about it. When the directors or managers of an institution set up an educational program, they believe certain results should be realized. They have expectations of what the program should accomplish. Now, the persons who are taking a direct part in the program, the group participants and the leaders and teachers, also anticipate certain conditions and results. Often the expectations of the various learners are quite different. If the program is

168

to succeed, the expectations of those who sponsor it and of those who participate in it must be reconciled to some degree.

We are concerned with teaching people. In every situation in adult education we are involved with people. All that is done is done to help people in one way or another. When it was discovered that certain ideas fitted together in a related pattern, the notion of "subject" was born. Since then, various subjects have been used as organized ways to transfer information from the teacher and the book to the learner. As a matter of convenience in communication, we speak of people teaching subjects. Often this is all too true. Leaders or teachers sometimes become more concerned with the area of knowledge in which their interest lies than they are with the people who seek that knowledge. In adult education we need to comprehend clearly the purpose of the subject and recognize that it is designed primarily to help people. We, therefore, emphasize that we teach people, not subjects.

Programs of adult education must be in keeping with the environment in which they exist. If the needs of the participants are carefully analyzed, it will be discovered that these needs emerge from the nature of the situations and problems that affect the adult learners. Programs must be indigenous. They must be intimately related to the environment that helps make the learner the kind of person he is. Such factors as nationalistic backgrounds, urban or rural views, education, religion, geographical location and all the influences these involve are vital points; to a significant degree, they will determine the nature of the program, its direction, and its extent. Programs must be adapted to the nature of the learner and to his problems.

Although programs should be indigenous, they need not be provincial. The circumscribed ideas often associated with institutional and geographical provincialism can distort the mind by inhibiting discovery and growth. Adult education programs should be designed to help learners move outward in their intellectual development, to extend their horizons, to expand their views.

Adult education should make a continuing attack on ignorance, disease, superstition, and enslavement of mind and spirit. Its purpose is to liberate people; to provide creative opportunities for utilizing their talents and energies; to help them learn to play their roles as dignified human beings and as citizens in a society in which they can have some control of the social forces operating on them; and to show them how to do all this with the intelligence and decorum that befit human dignity.

SELECTED READING LIST

Adler, Alfred. *Understanding Human Nature.* Tr. by W. Beran Wolfe. New York: Fawcett World Library (Premier R192), 1961, 244 pp.

Aristotle. *Politics.* Tr. by Benjamin Jowett. New York: Random House (Modern Library), 1943, 337 pp.

Bergevin, Paul, and McKinley, John. *Participation Training For Adult Education.* St. Louis: Bethany Press, 1965, 108 pp.

Bergevin, Paul, Morris, Dwight, and Smith, Robert M. *Adult Education Procedures.* New York: Seabury Press, 1963, 245 pp. (Paperback edition, 1966).

Breasted, James Henry. *A History of Egypt.* New York: Charles Scribner's Sons, 1909, 634 pp.

Brumbaugh, Robert S., and Lawrence, Nathaniel M. *Philosophers On Education.* Boston: Houghton Mifflin, 1963, 211 pp.

The Declaration of Independence.

Fromm, Erich. *The Art of Loving.* New York: Harper & Bros., 1956, 133 pp. (Paperback edition: New York: Bantam Books, H2563, 1963, 112 pp.)

Grattan, C. Hartley. *In Quest of Knowledge.* New York: Association Press, 1955, 337 pp.

Havighurst, Robert J. *Human Development and Education.* New York: Longmans, Green, 1953, 338 pp.

Havighurst, Robert J., and Orr, Betty. *Adult Education and Adult Needs.* Boston: Center for the Study of Liberal Education for Adults, 1956, 66 pp.

Hobbes, Thomas. *Leviathan.* Ed. by Frederick J. E. Woodbridge. New York: Charles Scribner's Sons, 1930, 418 pp.

Jefferson, Thomas. "First Inaugural Address." *The Life and Selected Writings of Thomas Jefferson.* Ed. by Adrienne Koch and William Peden. New York: Random House (Modern Library), 1944, 730 pp.

Kallen, Horace M. *Philosophical Issues in Adult Education.* Springfield, Ill.: Charles C. Thomas, 1962, 99 pp.

Kidd, J. R. *How Adults Learn.* New York: Association Press, 1959, 324 pp.

Koch, Hal. *Grundtvig.* Tr. by Llewellyn Jones. Yellow Springs, Ohio: Antioch Press, 1952, 201 pp.

Lawrence, Brother. *Brother Lawrence: On the Practice of the Presence of God.* Cincinnati: Forward Movement, 1941.

Lindeman, Eduard C. *The Meaning of Adult Education.* Montreal: Harvest House, 1961, 129 pp.

Locke, John. *An Essay Concerning Human Understanding.* New York: Macmillan (Collier Book), 1965, 413 pp.

Overstreet, Harry A. *The Mature Mind.* New York: W. W. Norton, 1949, 295 pp.

Rousseau, Jean Jacques. "The Social Contract." *The Social Contract and Discourses.* Tr. by G. D. H. Cole. New York: E. P. Dutton (Everyman's Library), 1950, 330 pp.

Smith, Thomas Vernor, and Lindeman, Eduard C. *The Democratic Way of Life.* New York: New American Library (Mentor MP356), 1961, 123 pp.

Whitehead, Alfred North. *The Aims of Education and Other Essays.* New York: Macmillan, 1959, 247 pp. (Paperback edition: New York: New American Library, Mentor MP373, 1964, 166 pp.)

Wilson, Woodrow. *The New Freedom.* Englewood Cliffs, N.J.: Prentice-Hall, 1961, 173 pp.

Index

Needs, adjust program to meet, 110
in effective programming, 141
indifference to, 141-143
manifestations of failure to consider, 142
failure to identify, 143
symptomatic, 144
felt, 145
real, 146
See also Adults

Participation training, description of, 56-57, 59
need for, 103
application of, 145
Philosophy, basic characteristics of, 3-4
summary, 5-6
assumption of, 8
opposing concepts, 17-18
relationship to processes and procedures, 65-66
a prime concept, 135
Pride, as a problem, 75 ff.
Problem areas, 69
Problem-centered learning, cf. Subject-centered learning, 148-149, 167
Professional study of adult education, 60 ff.
Programming, variety in, 25
related to needs, 141, 166
as a cooperative experience, 151 ff., 168
involvement of learners, 152
and authority, 154
and shared responsibility, 155-156
voluntary nature of sharing in, 166
appropriate resources for, 166
and problem-centered learning, 167
related to expectations, 168

a cooperative endeavor, 168
related to environment, 123 ff., 169
indigenous nature of, 169

Random learning, 26, 29, 33, 40, 59 ff.
characteristics of, 60
Republic, 112-113
Resistance to change, as a problem, 92 ff.
Resources, list of, 149
appropriateness of, 150-151, 166
persons as, 151
Rousseau, J. J., 34, 35

Schools, prime responsibility of, 15
feelings about, 49, 53-54
limitations, 90, 91
in adult education, 106
vocational nature of, 109
lack of trained leaders, 109
See also Formalized education
Self-esteem, as distinguished from pride, 78
Situation-centered learning, see Problem-centered learning
Social development, arrested, 75
Social order, industrialized, 24
urban, 24
directed by adults, 76
and education, 101-102
and change, 103
Society, nature of, 160
Subject-centered learning, cf. Problem-centered learning, 148,149
Subjects, 89 ff., 169
Survival, education for, 38-39
Systematic learning, 53 ff.
characteristics of, 58-59

Teaching-learning process, need for full participation in, 27

175